DATE DUE

FEDERALISM

Published in association with the Centre for Canadian Studies at Mount Allison University. Information on the Canadian Democratic Audit project can be found at www.CanadianDemocraticAudit.ca.

Advisory Group

William Cross, Director (Mount Allison University)
R. Kenneth Carty (University of British Columbia)
Elisabeth Gidengil (McGill University)
Richard Sigurdson (University of New Brunswick)
Frank Strain (Mount Allison University)
Michael Tucker (Mount Allison University)

Titles

John Courtney, *Elections*
William Cross, *Political Parties*
Elisabeth Gidengil, André Blais, Neil Nevitte, and Richard Nadeau, *Citizens*
Jennifer Smith, *Federalism*
Lisa Young and Joanna Everitt, *Advocacy Groups*
David Docherty, *Legislatures*
Darin Barney, *Communications Technology*
Ian Greene, *The Courts*
Graham White, *Cabinets and First Ministers*

FEDERALISM

Jennifer Smith

UBCPress

15 14 13 12 11 10 09 08 07 06 05 04   5 4 3 2 1

Printed in Canada on acid-free paper that is 100% post-consumer recycled, processed chlorine-free, and printed with vegetable-based, low-VOC inks.

Library and Archives Canada Cataloguing in Publication

Smith, Jennifer, 1950-
    Federalism / Jennifer Smith.

    (Canadian democratic audit ; 4)
    Includes bibliographical references and index.
    ISBN 0-7748-1101-3 (set). – ISBN 0-7748-1060-2

    1. Federal government – Canada. I. Title. II. Series.

JL27.S62 2004   320.471   C2004-904137-1

Canadä

UBC Press gratefully acknowledges the financial support for our publishing program of the Government of Canada through the Book Publishing Industry Development Program (BPIDP), and of the Canada Council for the Arts and the British Columbia Arts Council.

The Centre for Canadian Studies thanks the Harold Crabtree Foundation for its support of the Canadian Democratic Audit project.

UBC Press
The University of British Columbia
2029 West Mall
Vancouver, BC V6T 1Z2
604-822-5959 / Fax: 604-822-6083
www.ubcpress.ca

Contents

Foreword

This volume is part of the Canadian Democratic Audit series. The objective of this series is to consider how well Canadian democracy is performing at the outset of the twenty-first century. In recent years, political and opinion leaders, government commissions, academics, citizen groups, and the popular press have all identified a "democratic deficit" and "democratic malaise" in Canada. These characterizations often are portrayed as the result of a substantial decline in Canadians' confidence in their democratic practices and institutions. Indeed, Canadians are voting in record low numbers, many are turning away from the traditional political institutions, and a large number are expressing declining confidence in both their elected politicians and the electoral process.

Nonetheless, Canadian democracy continues to be the envy of much of the rest of the world. Living in a relatively wealthy and peaceful society, Canadians hold regular elections in which millions cast ballots. These elections are largely fair, efficient, and orderly events. They routinely result in the selection of a government with no question about its legitimate right to govern. Developing democracies from around the globe continue to look to Canadian experts for guidance in establishing electoral practices and democratic institutions. Without a doubt, Canada is widely seen as a leading example of successful democratic practice.

Given these apparently competing views, the time is right for a comprehensive examination of the state of Canadian democracy. Our purposes are to conduct a systematic review of the operations of Canadian democracy, to listen to what others have to say about Canadian democracy, to assess its strengths and weaknesses, to consider where there are opportunities for advancement, and to evaluate popular reform proposals.

A democratic audit requires the setting of benchmarks for evaluation of the practices and institutions to be considered. This necessarily involves substantial consideration of the meaning of democracy.

"Democracy" is a contested term and we are not interested here in striking a definitive definition. Nor are we interested in a theoretical model applicable to all parts of the world. Rather we are interested in identifying democratic benchmarks relevant to Canada in the twenty-first century. In selecting these we were guided by the issues raised in the current literature on Canadian democratic practice and by the concerns commonly raised by opinion leaders and found in public opinion data. We have settled on three benchmarks: public participation, inclusiveness, and responsiveness. We believe that any contemporary definition of Canadian democracy must include institutions and decision-making practices that are defined by public participation, that this participation include all Canadians, and that government outcomes respond to the views of Canadians.

While settling on these guiding principles, we have not imposed a strict set of democratic criteria on all of the evaluations that together constitute the Audit. Rather, our approach allows the auditors wide latitude in their evaluations. While all auditors keep the benchmarks of participation, inclusiveness, and responsiveness central to their examinations, each adds additional criteria of particular importance to the subject he or she is considering. We believe this approach of identifying unifying themes, while allowing for divergent perspectives, enhances the project by capturing the robustness of the debate surrounding democratic norms and practices.

We decided at the outset to cover substantial ground and to do so in a relatively short period. These two considerations, coupled with a desire to respond to the most commonly raised criticisms of the contemporary practice of Canadian democracy, result in a series that focuses on public institutions, electoral practices, and new phenomena that are likely to affect democratic life significantly. The series includes volumes that examine key public decision-making bodies: legislatures, the courts, and cabinets and government. The structures of our democratic system are considered in volumes devoted to questions of federalism and the electoral system. The ways in which citizens participate in electoral politics and policy making are a crucial component of the project, and thus we include studies of interest groups and political parties. The desire and capacity of Canadians for meaningful participation in public life is also the subject of a volume. Finally, the challenges and opportunities raised by new communication technologies are also considered. The Audit does not include studies devoted to the status of particular groups of Canadians. Rather than separate out Aboriginals, women, new Canadians, and others, these groups are treated together with all Canadians throughout the Audit.

In all, this series includes nine volumes examining specific areas of Canadian democratic life. A tenth, synthetic volume provides an overall assessment and makes sense out of the different approaches and findings found in the rest of the series. Our examination is not exhaustive. Canadian democracy is a vibrant force, the status of which can never be fully captured at one time. Nonetheless the areas we consider involve many of the pressing issues currently facing democracy in Canada. We do not expect to have the final word on this subject. Rather, we hope to encourage others to pursue similar avenues of inquiry.

A project of this scope cannot be accomplished without the support of many individuals. At the top of the list of those deserving credit are the members of the Canadian Democratic Audit team. From the very beginning, the Audit has been a team effort. This outstanding group of academics has spent many hours together, defining the scope of the project, prodding each other on questions of Canadian democracy, and most importantly, supporting one another throughout the endeavour, all with good humour. To Darin Barney, André Blais, Kenneth Carty, John Courtney, David Docherty, Joanna Everitt, Elisabeth Gidengil, Ian Greene, Richard Nadeau, Neil Nevitte, Richard Sigurdson, Jennifer Smith, Frank Strain, Michael Tucker, Graham White, and Lisa Young, I am forever grateful.

The Centre for Canadian Studies at Mount Allison University has been my intellectual home for several years. The Centre, along with the Harold Crabtree Foundation, has provided the necessary funding and other assistance necessary to see this project through to fruition. At Mount Allison University, Peter Ennals provided important support to this project when others were skeptical; Wayne MacKay and Michael Fox have continued this support since their respective arrivals on campus; and Joanne Goodrich and Peter Loewen have provided important technical and administrative help.

The University of British Columbia Press, particularly its senior acquisitions editor, Emily Andrew, has been a partner in this project from the very beginning. Emily has been involved in every important decision and has done much to improve the result. Camilla Gurdon has overseen the copyediting and production process and in doing so has made these books better. Scores of Canadian and international political scientists have participated in the project as commentators at our public conferences, as critics at our private meetings, as providers of quiet advice, and as referees of the volumes. The list is too long to name them all, but David Cameron, Sid Noel, Leslie Seidle, Jim Bickerton, Alexandra Dobrowolsky, Livianna Tossutti, Janice Gross Stein, and Frances Abele all deserve special recognition for their contributions. We are also grateful to the Canadian Study of Parliament Group, which partnered with us for our inaugural conference in Ottawa in November 2001.

Finally, this series is dedicated to all of the men and women who contribute to the practice of Canadian democracy. Whether as active participants in parties, groups, courts, or legislatures, or in the media and the universities, without them Canadian democracy would not survive.

William Cross
Director, The Canadian Democratic Audit
Sackville, New Brunswick

Acknowledgments

I would like to thank William Cross, the editor of the Canadian Democratic Audit series, for the opportunity to explore the theme of federalism and democracy in Canada; my fellow authors in the series for helping me to clarify various ideas; and the people at UBC Press for their editorial assistance. I am grateful to the anonymous readers of my draft, whose comments on it were immensely useful to me. All mistakes are mine alone.

Federalism

AUDITING FEDERALISM IN CANADA 1

In these early years of the twenty-first century, disenchantment with democracy is growing in Canada. It is telling that the disenchantment is not confined to a few academics in the ivory tower. It finds expression in the editorial pages of the newspapers; in the neighbourhood communities struggling to save their schools from the chopping block; among the protestors on the streets who oppose globalization; and among members of Parliament who find themselves with nothing useful to contribute to the policy-making process. Even senior political figures make easy reference to the "democratic deficit," the catch-all phrase now used to describe the problem.

Since Canada is classed as one of the world's democracies, as well as one of the top countries in which to live, one can be forgiven for wondering what exactly is the problem here. While it is impossible to be sure, the problem appears to be dissatisfaction with the traditional practice of democracy. The traditional practice can be summed up in the term "representation." Canadians possess a representative form of democracy. For the most part unquestioned for decades, representative democracy is now held by many to be inadequate, insufficient, or simply not democratic enough. Canadians also live under a federal system of government. The question addressed in this volume is whether federalism is part of the democratic problem or part of the solution to the problem. Before turning to federalism, however, it is worth considering representative democracy a little further.

Representation is the key to Canada's democracy and every other democracy in the world. In its simplest form, democracy means a government in which the people rule rather than one person or a few. For the people to rule, they must be political equals. Representation enters the picture when the people choose not to govern themselves directly but instead to elect individuals to govern them. Those who are elected are said to represent the people and to have a mandate from the people to govern them. The people get to hold them accountable for their record of governing at the next election.

One clear reason for using representative democracy rather than direct democracy is population size. The oldest democracies – usually referred to as liberal democracies – are mass societies. To cite an extreme case, the United States has a population of 290 million and rising. Even Canada, with a mere 31.6 million souls, exhibits the phenomenon of population density because so many of them live in a few metropolitan centres scattered across the country. The election of a tiny number of individuals to govern seems an obvious way to organize a democracy in such circumstances. Even in a technocratic era that permits telephone or Internet voting, the citizenry as a whole cannot be involved directly in governing on anything other than an intermittent basis. But there is a price to pay for representative democracy, and the price is less democracy. Representative democracy is a highly organized, structured affair. This is true whether it takes the form of the Canadian parliamentary system, the American congressional system, or the mixed parliamentary-presidential system used in France. In the end a very few individuals end up doing the governing, which makes the system elitist. The phrase "democratic elitism" is sometimes used to describe this situation.

Democratic elitism is not necessarily or inherently intolerable, although the formal structures of government are indeed exclusive rather than inclusive. In Canada until recently, there were only 301 elected members of Parliament, each representing an electoral district or riding. A small percentage of them will become cabinet ministers, and one the prime minister. The number of ridings – and therefore members – was increased to 308 in time for the 2004 general election, in accordance with the representation formula currently in use. In the US Congress, which consists of the Senate and the House of Representatives, the Senate comprises only two senators elected from each state, while the House seats 435 members elected in accordance with the population of the states. There is one president. The obvious exclusiveness of such systems is made tolerable by various formal rules and informal processes. Among the formal rules are regular elections; voter equality or one person, one vote; free and fair electoral procedures, including the use of the secret ballot; open competition among candidates for office; and the establishment and maintenance of individual freedoms, like the freedoms of speech and association that enable public debate and criticism, especially criticism of the politicians. Then there are the informal processes.

The informal processes are so called because they are not required by the law in the way that, say, courts and legislatures are required to exist. They might, however, be regulated by the law. The informal processes are the ways in which citizens communicate for political purposes with one another and with the elected politicians. They do so through political parties (see Cross 2004) and through interest groups and social movements (see Young and Everitt 2004). Their strategies range from quiet consultations held behind the scenes to efforts to influence public opinion through the media to open protest on the streets – and everything in between. The informal processes flourish, in part, because of the political freedoms of expression and association that are the standard requirements of liberal democracies everywhere.

Legal rules and informal processes can help to modify the elitist nature of representative democracy – to democratize it, so to speak. Nonetheless, some elitist features of the system can harden, a tendency that frustrates citizens' democratic expectations, which are reputed to be higher than ever (Nevitte 1996). Examples abound of these hardened arteries that contribute to the democratic deficit. The centre of power in the federal government is said to be concentrated more and more in the office of the prime minister (see White 2005; Savoie 1999). MPs, who are the political representatives of the people, appear to have little role in the making of public policy (see Docherty 2004). They even have a tough time representing the views of constituents when those do not coincide with the position of the political party to which they belong. The political parties are the organizational anchor of the parliamentary system in Canada and in Parliament they are highly disciplined, probably the most disciplined of any in the countries that use the parliamentary system. This gives MPs little room to act independently of the parties on behalf of their constituents. All of this makes the system hard for ordinary citizens to penetrate. Of course they can easily join a political party, but that is hardly a guarantee of influence over public policy. On the contrary, the successful political parties are essentially vehicles for choosing the party leader, not for engaging the members in policy deliberation.

Despite much talk about the democratic possibilities of the technological revolution in communications, this revolution has not led to a closer relationship between the citizens and the government or even between the citizens and the political parties. There are no e-voting developments of any note. Secrecy exists everywhere in government, so that citizens often are forced to use the slow processes of the law to ferret out even mundane bits of information. Meanwhile, some interests – the big battalions, like business and professional organizations – appear to have more access to the government than others – like environmentalists and antipoverty groups. This inequality persists despite the efforts that the government makes from time to time to consult widely with Canadians. In addition to the established interests, newer identity communities based on gender or sexual orientation find themselves inadequately represented in the political institutions. And old identities as well, notably the Aboriginal communities, have been long unrepresented and marginalized and only now, with the help of the courts, are beginning to carve out some self-governing space for themselves.

The dilemma of representative democracy in Canada today, then, is how to invigorate it. Representative democracy is not going away.

The 31.6 million Canadians are not about to engage in a fury of direct self-government. The chaos would be unbearable. And in any event most people believe they have better things to do, like earning a living or pursuing their pleasures. They would rather leave the governing to the elected representatives and the public servants. Public dissatisfaction with the current system cannot be ignored, however. All parts of the system, including federalism, need close analysis in order for us to get a clear grasp of the reasons for this dissatisfaction and what can be done to improve matters. That close analysis is the function of this democratic audit.

An audit requires instruments of measurement. The democratic audit under way in this series uses the concepts of inclusiveness, participation, and responsiveness to measure the robustness of the country's democratic life. Inclusiveness raises the issue of which citizens are likely to be included in political and governmental activities and which citizens are not likely to be included in them. In other words, who is in? Citizens need not participate in political life, but should they choose to participate then they need to know what they can do. Participation refers to the kinds of activities in which citizens can engage should they be so inclined. What can they do? Responsiveness refers to governments. The concern is the extent to which governments can respond to the demands and concerns of the citizens and the ways in which governments respond. What can the citizens expect?

While public attention – and dissatisfaction – is often focused on institutions in the news such as Parliament and the office of the prime minister, it must be recalled that many other institutions and processes are crucial to the quality of democratic life in the country, such as the electoral system, the political parties, interest groups, and the judicial system, to name a few. Our system of government is complex, being composed of interrelated elements, each of which is subject to this audit. One of these elements is federalism.

Canada has a federal system of government, which means it has a lot of governments. Canadians deal with municipal or local governments, provincial and territorial governments, Aboriginal governments, and the federal government. Being used to this state of affairs, Canadians probably see nothing odd about the federal system at all. Indeed, given the vast size of the country and the heterogeneity of the population, they might say that it would hardly do to organize the governing system any other way. They might even wonder why it merits a book. But federalism is relevant to Canadians because it is relevant to the quality of their democracy. Obviously the federal system has an impact on the country's democratic life. Common sense alone would suggest as much. One of the purposes of this volume is to identify systematically the ways in which the federal system affects democracy. This is not as easy as it might look, however, mainly because federalism is not a fixed and exact thing.

Federalism should be fixed and exact. After all, it can be defined under the Constitution in terms of levels of government, each armed with specified powers and responsibilities. Despite this legal precision, however, federalism has a fluid, even elusive quality. For one reason, there is no one, perfect type against which all others can be measured. There is no standard. Instead there is a range of federal systems, each uniquely composed of a different package of features. For another reason, the democratic credentials of federalism are contested, some analysts seeing democratic virtues and others seeing undemocratic flaws, both looking at the same thing, of course. The reason for the contest is that federalism is a structure with the potential to enhance democracy or to diminish it. Which way federalism leans depends a great deal on the way that political and bureaucratic actors, and citizens, use the structure.

The democratic audit can tell us how federalism is used in Canada now. By applying the concepts of inclusiveness, participation, and responsiveness, the audit can tell us whether the federal system enhances or diminishes democracy. Does federalism encourage an inclusive democratic process? Does federalism serve to boost the participation of citizens in democratic politics? Does federalism enhance the prospect that governments will be more responsive to citizens than they would be in the absence of federalism? These are the questions that need to asked and answered in order to assess the democratic credentials of federalism.

In preparation for the audit, Chapter 2 offers some important background considerations about federalism. The oldest federal systems are identified, and the common definition of the term is developed at some length. Then the origins of the earliest modern federal system – the United States – are reviewed briefly. Federalism as we know it is an American product, and therefore it is instructive to inquire whether the Americans latched on to the idea of federalism in order to pursue democratic objectives or for other reasons. Some writers say that there were other reasons, and that in any event the federal structure has antidemocratic aspects. In contrast, other writers contend that, origins notwithstanding, the federal structure is well suited to the enhancement of democracy. These alternative lines of thought are explored in the chapter.

Once the antidemocratic and democratic possibilities of the federal structure have been laid out, we turn to the Canadian system, which is the subject of Chapter 3. Canadian federalism is a slippery business, not just because it is full of quirks and peculiarities but because it is both changing and unchanging, both in flux and in cement. In order to undertake an accurate democratic audit of it, it is vital to distinguish between the changeable aspects of the system, on the one hand, and the patterns or institutions that never seem to change, on the other. The chapter begins with a salutary reminder of the thinking of the leading figures at Confederation on the subject of democracy and then shows how that thinking is reflected in the central features of their handiwork, the country's federal Constitution.

The audit itself is the subject of the next three chapters, which are devoted to the measures of inclusiveness, participation, and responsiveness. Chapter 4 analyzes how Canadian federalism includes citizens in political life and how it works to exclude them. Chapter 5 analyzes the ways in which Canadian federalism encourages those who are included to participate in politics and the ways in which it discourages them from doing so. In Chapter 6, on the responsiveness of governments, the issue is whether the dynamic of the relationship between governments that the federal structure establishes has the effect of making them more responsible to the citizens or not.

Chapter 7 summarizes where Canadian federalism stands in terms of the audit, and suggests that it could do with a little more democratization. But not a lot more. This is where the discussion in Chapter 2 on the antidemocratic and democratic potentials of federalism bears fruit, in setting parameters for the democratic expectations of federalism that Canadians can reasonably maintain. The proposals advanced here are few in number, but they are aimed at making the system more inclusive without incapacitating it; at enabling the included to participate more in the conduct of political life without immobilizing it; and at exacting more responsiveness from the elected governments to the electors, without requiring the governments to pander to public fads and fashions any more than they do now.

While few in number, these proposals are bound to be challenged not only on their merits but on the grounds of feasibility. Readers will want to know if there is any realistic possibility of implementing them. Accordingly, Chapter 8 discusses the challenges to be faced in making changes to the federal system to make it more democratic. In fact, the challenges are enormous. It is extremely difficult to get widespread agreement on proposed changes to the federal system in a country as large and diverse as Canada. The last attempt was the referendum on the Charlottetown Accord in 1992, which failed. The Charlottetown Accord aimed at sweeping changes to the federation. As is argued here, a limited number of carefully crafted proposals might prove a better bet, especially if they are driven by the desire to improve Canadian democracy *and* Canadian federalism. In other words, they must reach federalism through reforms to enhance democracy.

FEDERALISM AND DEMOCRACY 2

Is federalism democratic? Some very astute theorists of federalism answer no, and some equally astute theorists answer yes. A review of the arguments on both sides will help to deepen the understanding of federalism, add a dash of realism to expectations about the extent to which federalism supports democracy, and set the stage for the democratic audit of federalism. But first, some definitions must be clarified at the outset in order to avoid confusion later. Accordingly, this chapter begins with the commonly held definitions of federalism and the federal system of government. Then the key structural features of the federal system of government are identified and explored.

Federalism

The federal idea of an agreement or treaty that binds political communities in a larger whole is as old as the Greek city states that banded together to protect themselves against an external military threat. Federalism as it is known today, however, is no older than the American federal system (Finer 1932, 244), which was followed by Switzerland (1848), Canada (1867), Australia (1901), Austria (1920), and Germany (1949). These six are the oldest of the genre, although

India (1950) followed quickly. A recent example is Belgium (1993). Spain (1978) is regarded as a federation in fact, if not in law. All of these countries have highly developed industrial and technological societies. But there are federations in the developing world, too, such as Malaysia (1963). Finally, there are failed federations, two recent and spectacular examples being the former Czechoslovakia and the former Yugoslavia.

The tragedy of failed federations is the tragedy of the failure of peaceful, democratic coexistence. It is like the failure of a dream. "Federalism" is an honourable term in political science, with positive connotations. The word is derived from the Latin *foedus*, which means faith. The Latin root suggests the friendship or the faith in one another that political communities express when they decide to join together in a federation or federal system of government. Clearly, the term has positive connotations. It suggests that there is value in communities joining together for some purposes while at the same time retaining their independence for other purposes. It suggests that there can be diversity in unity. It recommends the combination of shared government and self-government.

The related terms "federation" and "federal system of government" describe the kind of governmental arrangement that federalism implies. In a federal system, the participating political communities agree to pursue some objectives together and other objectives on their own. More specifically, they agree to establish a central government and to empower it to make and administer laws in some areas; and they agree to retain the power to make and administer laws themselves in other areas. The laws of the central government apply to the residents of the federation as a whole. The laws of the federating communities – the provinces or states or subunits, terms that vary from federation to federation – apply to those who live within their respective boundaries. One of the leading students of federalism, Ronald Watts (1999a, 1), describes this essential feature of the federal system of government as "a combination of shared-rule for some purposes and regional self-rule for others within a single political system so that neither is subordinate to the other."

The last words in the preceding quotation – "so that neither is sub-ordinate to the other" – capture a second essential feature of the fed-eral system. The central government is not subordinate to the local governments, and the local governments are not subordinate to the central government. Instead, there is an equality between them because each level of government – central and local – is independent within the sphere of work that is assigned to it. This independence does not mean that in a federal system the two levels of government need to be equally empowered. They need not be and are not. Some federal systems are said to be centralized, which means that the cen-tral government is stronger and busier than the local governments. Other federal systems are said to be decentralized, which means that the local governments are stronger and busier than the central gov-ernment. The point is that each level of government has autonomous decision-making power within the areas assigned to it, whether these areas be large or small. In this respect, federations must be distin-guished from unitary systems, like France, that employ local govern-ments to help administer policies that are made by the central gov-ernment. The French use a system of administrative decentralization, not a federal system of government.

In addition to the type of equality that exists between the two lev-els of government is the type of equality among the local governments themselves, particularly in the older federations. The local govern-ments are equals with each other, at least in the sense that each pos-sesses the same law-making powers in the same assigned areas. Thus in Canada, Prince Edward Island possesses the same set of powers and responsibilities as Ontario, Quebec, or Alberta. Obviously PEI is a small island with a tiny population and a modest economy by compar-ison with those three provinces, which are geographically large, pop-ulous, and wealthy. There is no territorial, demographic, or economic equality here. The equality among them resides only in the fact that under the Constitution their governments are treated the same. It should be stressed that this measure of equality – or symmetry – is not as common in new, emerging federations (like Spain) as it is in the older federations.

All of this points to a third important feature of a federal system, namely, that it is a legal construct. A federal system is always rooted in a treaty or a constitution, in other words, a written agreement. The governments of the federation derive their powers and responsibilities from the constitution. As a result, the importance of the written constitution can hardly be overstated. Disputes between the governments are often disputes about the meaning of the constitution. If they do not begin that way, they often become that way. Unsurprisingly, then, federations use courts as umpires of disputes between governments when the governments themselves are unable to resolve them on their own (see Greene 2005). Of course there are other mechanisms to deal with such disputes: constitutions can be amended, or the citizens can be consulted in an election or a referendum vote. Nevertheless, as a rule the courts handle disputes between governments about the constitution. The parties to a dispute are expected to abide by the ruling of the courts. Thus the rule of law is a powerful norm or underlying value of federal systems of government.

Reference has been made to the amendment of the constitution, that is, the formal process under which the terms of the constitution are changed. This process is a significant feature of federal systems, even if it is rarely used – or rather, precisely because it is rarely used. Constitutions, being expected to endure, are generally made difficult to change, a fact that indicates the seriousness and earnestness with which the parties enter into them. The details of the amendment process vary from federation to federation. Nevertheless, the one common theme is the need for widespread agreement for change. No federation permits one of the governments to amend anything important in the constitution unilaterally, that is, on its own.

Finally, there is the issue of the representation of the units of the federation in the central government. Probably the best-known example is the Senate of the United States. The Senate is the upper house of the Congress, the legislative branch of the US national government. In each of the states of the United States the voters elect two senators to the Senate. This is a dramatic illustration of the principle of the equality of the states. In the Senate it trumps the rival principle of representation by population – one person, one vote – which is used as the basis of election to the House of Representatives, the lower house of the Congress. However influential the American example might be, few other federations follow it. Indeed, the variation in the way that the member states are represented in the national government is striking, although they are always represented in some fashion or other.

The formal features that distinguish the federal system of government from other systems, then, can be summarized as follows:

1 the combination of shared rule (a central government that deals with general matters and makes laws applicable to all of the citizens) and local self-rule (local governments that deal with local matters and make laws for the residents within their boundaries)
2 the constitutionally protected autonomy of each level of government, central and local
3 a written constitution and courts that are empowered with the authority to settle disputes arising under it
4 a constitutional amending formula that is designed to prevent any one government of the federation from making changes to the constitution unilaterally
5 a central government that is designed in part to represent the units of the federation.

It is essential not to lose sight of the concrete factor that underlies these five features and anchors all federal systems today: territoriality. The communities that join together to form a federal state are not virtual communities but land-based communities. They inhabit territory that is demarcated by boundaries. A quick glance at a map of Canada shows the boundaries of the provinces and territories that together make up the country. Thus the local governments referred to in the list above are invariably governments of territorially defined units, be they provinces (as in Canada), states (as in the United States), Länder (as in Germany), or cantons (as in Switzerland).

For the sake of completeness, it is useful to wind up this discussion of definitions by distinguishing the federal system from the unitary system or union, on the one hand, and the confederal system or confederation, on the other. As noted above, in a unitary system like France's (or New Zealand's or Israel's), there is one general government and no other governments empowered independently of it. Local or municipal governments may be established for purposes of administration, but these entities are not independent actors. Until recently, Great Britain was regarded as the classic example of a unitary state. Sovereignty resided in the British Parliament, period. And while there was and remains a strong tradition of local government, the tradition was a matter of Parliament's pleasure. Britain is now experimenting with the permanent devolution of power to Wales and Scotland, and this development means that the country can no longer be classified as unitary. Instead, it is moving in the direction of a federal system.

The confederal system, by contrast, is at the other extreme, since it features powerful constituent governments and a weak central government that is dependent upon them. In this system the constituent governments establish the central government and assign some responsibilities to it. They also control it because it is made up of the delegates that they send to it. The first government of the United States under the Articles of Confederation, which lasted from 1777 to 1789, was a confederation. Today, the European Union is the leading example of a confederation. Currently the EU comprises fifteen European states, with several others waiting in the wings to join. Although the EU has adopted some features that are designed to strengthen the independence of its central institutions, these institutions remain subject to the direction of the member countries.

Realist Origins of Federalism

As even a quick glance at the formal features listed above suggests, federal systems of government are highly structured affairs. They reveal a definite legal architecture that is made up of various rules and processes. Some might wonder whether the complexity is worth the bother, or even how federal systems got started.

At the risk of oversimplification, it can be stated that this question has a realist answer and an idealist answer. The realist answer was given by William Riker, who argued that federalism is the alternative to empire. To use his words, "Federalism is the main alternative to empire as a technique of aggregating large areas under one government" (Riker 1964, 5). It is worth pausing to consider this further.

Riker took the view that, even in this presumably enlightened age, governments — or enough of them, at any rate — like to preside over large territories. They want to grow, not shrink. The reasons are obvious. Territorial expansion is equated with greater wealth and enhanced military capacity. And technological advances in transportation and communications continue to make expansion a practical prospect. The old route to power and riches was imperialism, the assembling of the great empires, mostly through force. But empires are expensive to maintain and have a habit of collapsing, and imperialism is discredited today in any case. Enter federalism, which offered a new route to territorial aggrandizement accomplished by agreement rather than by force.

If nothing else, this throws a fresh light on federalism, and suggests that we ought not to view it entirely through rose-coloured glasses. Riker tested his views by examining the origins of a number of federations including, incidentally, Canada's. He found these federations to originate in a constitutional "bargain" struck between the likely leaders of the new federation and the leaders of the constituent governments contemplating entry into the federation. He argued that the political leaders who offer the bargain want to expand their territorial control for either economic or military reasons or both. But these same leaders are not prepared to use force to expand, either because they are unable to do so or because they prefer not to for ideological reasons — possibly they are democrats. The political leaders who consider the offer do so either for defensive reasons, being concerned about potential aggressors, or because they want to participate in opportunities vouchsafed by the larger federation. They are prepared to trade some decision-making powers for safety or for economic opportunities or both.

Immediately noticeable in the Riker analysis is the omission of democracy. Yet federalism is not a product of military conquest; it involves negotiation among presumed equals. It is an alternative to empire, not a duplicate of empire. Therefore the federal system of government is not inherently incompatible with democracy, even for someone like Riker, who sees in its origins no concern for democracy. Riker, however, made the claim that the federal bargain is not struck in order to promote democracy. This insight is valuable not because it is true, but because it might be true. If the federal bargain is not struck in order to promote democracy, then maybe it does not promote it.

Following Riker's insight, then, it is wise to ask whether the federal system of government has the effect of impeding or standing in the way of democracy. And the only way federalism could do that, presumably, is by blocking the will of the majority sometimes. One of the leading liberals of the nineteenth century, John Dalberg-Acton — almost always referred to as Lord Acton — recommended federalism because he thought it had precisely that effect. His is another argument worth considering.

FEDERALISM BLOCKS THE WILL OF THE MAJORITY

Acton based his argument on a reading of American federalism. He studied the work of the Philadelphia convention in 1787, at which the federal constitution was drafted, and the conduct of American government and politics under the constitution. He was also a student of the Civil War. He became a great admirer of the principle of federalism authored by the Americans, largely because he found it to be a congenial, effective, and peaceful way of restraining democracy.

By democracy, Acton meant government action that is based on the will of the majority, or majority rule. Acton thought that the majority often needed to be restrained from oppressing the minority, and in American federalism he saw a new and powerful restraint. The chief mechanism was the division of powers between the Congress, on the one hand, and the states, on the other. The Congress could represent the will of the majority only in relation to the subjects of legislation assigned to it under the constitution. The states could represent the will of the majority within their boundaries only in relation to the rest – or the reserve power – that is, what was not assigned to the Congress. Right away, then, federalism places a constraint on the capacity of majorities to form and to dominate over those with different opinions. It sets up many majorities – majorities in the states as well as a national majority. The many majorities can easily cancel out one another.

Another mechanism of American federalism that Acton identified as a restraint on the will of the majority was the makeup of the Congress itself. Only the House of Representatives, he noted, was elected on the basis of representation by population and therefore able to represent national majorities. The Senate, being comprised of two senators per state, was not constructed to reflect national majorities, but instead to represent the states, giving each state the same voting power in that body irrespective of the size of its population. Such were the features of the American federal system that compelled Acton (1985, 211) to write glowingly about federalism as the "true natural check on absolute democracy" and the "one immortal tribute of America to political science."

FEDERALISM FRUSTRATES NONTYRANNOUS MAJORITIES

An easy rejoinder to Acton is that democracy should be understood to include more than majority rule. It should be understood to include the very things – like guaranteed rights and freedoms and institutional checks and balances – that he described as counters to majority tyranny. Then his argument is beside the point, because it is directed at the extreme case of majority tyranny that could not arise in a properly designed democracy. Yet the fact of the matter is that Acton saw in the structure of federalism a conservative bias. And while he valued that bias, not everyone can be expected to agree.

What about majorities that are not tyrannous? What about majorities that are collected within a system of guaranteed rights and freedoms? What about a strong popular will to undertake particular public policies that is continually frustrated by the checks inherent in the federal structure of government?

Disillusionment with federalism as an ongoing barrier to effective, vigorous government supported by well-meaning majorities as opposed to tyrannous ones has been expressed at different times over many years. One of the first to denounce this perceived effect of federalism was the influential nineteenth-century British constitutional scholar, A.V. Dicey. Dicey was an expert on the British governmental system, which he eulogized. Britain then was the classic unitary state in which sovereignty resided exclusively in the British Parliament. Understandably, the British model was the standard against which he compared other governments, in particular, the American system.

On the basis of his study of American federalism, Dicey (1893, 161) reached the conclusion that "federal government means weak government." He was convinced of this for several reasons, the most obvious being the time and energy wasted in the conflicts that were bound to erupt between the two levels of government. Governments wound up fighting each other, he wrote, rather than attending to the problems at hand. Another reason for the weakness of the system was the need of the central government to respond to the demands of the regions, or at least to be seen to respond to them. Unlike the British government, the government in Washington was unable easily to articulate a single national policy for the country as a whole, he wrote, but instead was compelled to take into account the conflicting demands of the states. The design of the Senate ensured such a result. Finally, he disapproved of the role of the courts in the resolution of disputes arising out of the written constitution.

Dicey found the written constitution to be a rigid instrument with a conservative effect on government. He thought that Americans were caught up in a kind of cult of the constitution that led them to revere the existing principles and institutions of the constitution at the expense of innovation and efficiency. Moreover, the central role of lawyers and judges in the adjudication of disputes about the constitution spelled a legalistic approach to the constitution that was bound to be restrictive and narrow, and to prize accepted practices above governmental flexibility. However his argument about American federalism is judged, in Canada the experience of the Depression appeared to many to illustrate Dicey's point admirably.

Before 1949, when appeals to it were abolished, a British body, the Judicial Committee of the Privy Council, was Canada's highest court of appeal. As the decades of the twentieth century passed, the Judicial Committee increasingly drew the ire of critics who regarded its approach to the interpretation of the Canadian Constitution as rigid, unimaginative, and scholastic. They accused it of treating the Constitution like an ordinary statute rather than the vehicle of the nation. Events came to a head in the Great Depression, when strapped provincial governments and unemployed Canadians looked to the federal government for economic assistance – in vain. The Judicial Committee struck down a number of social and economic programs enacted by Parliament on the ground that they were beyond its legislative competence under the Constitution (Laskin 1964). Eventually the Committee retreated from this position and began to develop a broader view of the constitutional capabilities of the federal government in meeting economic challenges. In other words, it changed its mind about the meaning of the Constitution. Nevertheless, for Canadians who sought government action during the worst economic crisis in the country's history, Dicey's warning about the legal straitjacket of federalism proved only too well founded.

CANADIAN FEDERALISM ENCOURAGES GOVERNMENTAL ELITISM

The Canadian economist Albert Breton (1985) offers a contemporary twist on the argument that federalism inhibits the responsiveness of governments to popular opinion, and it centres on the relationship between the federal government and the provincial governments. In a nutshell, his contention is that when governments compete with one another, they serve the people; when they work together, they work against the people.

In order to follow Breton's contention, we must distinguish between classical federalism and cooperative federalism. Under the classical model, which prevailed in Canada until the end of the Second World War, each level of government attends to its own business. There is little overlap of legislative responsibilities and therefore little need for structures of collaboration between the governments. The alternative cooperative model of federalism developed after the war as the federal government took the lead in establishing the foundations of the welfare state (Simeon and Robinson 1990, 129-53). The federal government needed the assistance of the provinces in this endeavour, since the provinces are responsible for matters like health and welfare. Over the years, then, consultative structures developed between elected officials and public servants from both levels of government. The adjective "cooperative" conveys the sense of such activity undertaken in an amiable spirit.

Of course, all was not amiable. At times there appeared to be as much intergovernmental strife as anything else. Thus a leading student of Canadian federalism, Donald Smiley, coined the phrase "executive federalism" to describe the machinery of federalism, cooperative or not. He defined executive federalism as "the relations between elected and appointed officials of the two orders of government in federal-provincial interactions and among the executives of the provinces in interprovincial interactions" (Smiley 1980, 91). This succinct definition makes no mention of the public. Instead, the system has the unmistakable whiff of elitism. Meetings are usually conducted behind closed doors; it is difficult for anyone other than insiders to know what is going on; and the public is relegated to the passive role of recipient of whatever results are transmitted to it. The few public meetings between elected leaders – the summits – have a stage-managed air about them, and generally are carefully orchestrated by officials behind the scenes.

Breton's argument is that the Canadian version of cooperative federalism — executive federalism — spoils the promise of democratic openness and responsiveness that is inherent in classical federalism. Under classical federalism, he contends, the stage is set for governments to compete for the affections of their respective publics, since no elected government wants to be upstaged by another. Moreover, when governments act on their own authority, as they do in classical federalism, the lines of accountability to their respective publics are clear. Once governments engage in extensive collaboration, however, they retreat into a process of ongoing consultations with each other that is difficult for the public to penetrate. The joint product they eventually produce negates the lines of accountability that the federal structure sets up in the first place. In other words, there is as much collusion as collaboration. It is important to stress that Breton is critical of the executive federalism that Canadians have developed, not of federalism per se. On the contrary, in his view federalism rightly understood and pursued — in other words, the classical model of federalism — establishes the competitive framework that is a key condition of an open democracy.

Such are the main arguments in support of the claim that federalism works against democracy. To summarize, Acton welcomed federalism as an antidote to the will of the majority, by which he often seemed to mean the tyranny of the majority. Dicey was a critic of federalism, seeing in it a structure that divides the power of government among central and regional units, thereby preventing any one of them from representing fully the people as a whole and on that basis being capable of strong action. He thought that federalism spells weak government. Breton inveighs against the Canadian version of federalism — executive federalism — on the ground that it stifles the open competition among governments for the support of the citizens that classical federalism is admirably designed to promote.

Each of these arguments raises some useful concerns about the impact of federalism on democracy. Neither Acton's nor Breton's proves, however, that federalism is inherently hostile to democracy. Acton's can be set aside on the ground that his definition of democracy as the rule of the majority is simply too narrow, and needs to be supplemented by other considerations. Breton's concern can be set aside – at least for now – because it arises out of his study of Canadian federalism rather than federalism generally. Breton does not think that federalism is inherently antidemocratic. His complaint is that the Canadian version of executive federalism has antidemocratic tendencies. That leaves Dicey, whose argument is critical to the democratic audit because it strikes at the democratic credentials of federalism.

Dicey's concern about federalism serving to obstruct the development of the will of the majority, and thereby producing weak government, is a general argument applicable to all federal systems. Moreover, it speaks to the factor of territoriality that, as noted earlier in the chapter, is the foundation of federal systems. For Dicey, the territorial communities obstruct the development of national majorities. In the context of Canadian federalism, the point is that the very existence of the provinces and the provincial governments, and the territories and the territorial governments, complicates the ability of the national government to develop national majorities in favour of public-policy agendas. For one thing, the provincial governments might work against the national government, attempting to mobilize provincial majorities against national initiatives that they oppose. A recent example (pursued in Chapter 6) involves the environmental agreement known as the Kyoto Protocol. The Alberta government was strongly opposed to the country's adoption of the accord, and mobilized considerable support in the province for its position. In the end, the federal government prevailed, but not without considerable effort.

Notwithstanding the power of Dicey's argument, it is not conclusive empirically because the world's federations are also among the world's liberal democracies, a fact of considerable significance. Thus it is worth considering how other theorists think that federalism works to support democracy. Their arguments are rooted in the idealist view of the origins of federalism.

Idealist Origins of Federalism

W.S. Livingston was one of the first students of federalism to insist on the importance of studying the society of any federal state. Livingston (1956, 21) wrote that the essence of federalism lies in the society itself, in particular, in the diverse communities that make up the society. In his view it is this diversity that necessitates a federal system in the first place. Consequently the formal, institutional features of any federal system are the product and the reflection of a particular social state of affairs.

Diversity is multifaceted. Many things can distinguish communities one from the other: linguistic, religious, and ethnic differences; economic differences so marked as to generate distinct ways of life; or lesser differences that have grown significant over time. The important feature of these communities in a federal system, however, is territory. This point was established earlier in the chapter and needs to be emphasized again. Only territorially based communities matter in federalism. The fact that the communities are territorially based gives them the shape and resilience to demand a measure of self-government.

Livingston saw federalism as the outcome of a contest between those who seek to aggregate communities into a unified state, and the community leaders who insist on some autonomy for the communities. Federalism is a compromise between autonomy and unity. "The federal system is thus an institutionalization of the compromise between these two demands," he wrote, "and the federal constitution draws the lines of this compromise" (1971, 26). He does not explain why the communities would want to join together, as Riker does. Rather he explains why they want to retain a measure of the autonomy that they already possess: in order to protect the very differences that make their communities what they are. The insistence on local autonomy drives the compromise that is federalism.

The idealist account of the origins of federalism contains the link between federalism and democracy. The federal structure has appeal for the diverse communities that choose to join together to form a larger entity. This is especially so when these communities are democratic themselves. In the case of most modern federations, the communities forming them have possessed some democratic credentials from the start. This is not to say that federal systems are *inherently* democratic. For example, Preston King (1982, 89) writes that while they are constitutional, lawful systems of government, they are not necessarily fully democratic. Daniel Elazar (1985) takes a stronger position, arguing that federal systems need not be democratic or constitutional. An example is the United Arab Emirates (UAE), which he describes as a federation of absolutist states, with autocratic rulers at the local level and in the central government. The purpose of this federation is to enable local rulers to share in the power of the central government. In Elazar's view, however, the UAE is the exception that proves the rule that federal systems are democratic. Federal systems are always established in the name of democracy, he argues, if not in the service of it. He cites the Soviet Union – in existence at the time he was writing – as an example of a democratic federation in name, if not in fact (Elazar 1985, 33). The Soviet Union's successor state, the Russian Federation, too, is a democratic federation in name but not in fact.

Students of federalism agree, then, that the nondemocratic federations are the exceptions that prove the rule. The rule is that diverse, democratic communities are bound to find the federal structure congenial to democracy. First and foremost, the federal structure offers them a way of staying intact and maintaining a measure of self-rule. Second, it offers them a central government in which they have some say, although not necessarily an equal say. Less obvious, perhaps, is the democratizing effect of another important feature of federalism, namely, the rule of law. The following sections explore the democratic weight of these three features of federalism.

Federalism, Autonomy, and Self-Rule

The ease with which federal systems accommodate the self-government of participating communities supports and encourages democracy in specific ways. The first and most obvious is the appeal of local auton-omy to local democrats. The communities that decide to establish a federation are not interested in union, otherwise they would form one. They want some of the benefits of a union, but they want some independent decision-making room, too. And they get it, often in rela-tion to policy areas that are particularly salient to their residents. The autonomy that the communities enjoy within the federation is more than a signal of the commitment to the decentralization of power. It is also an invitation to local communities to govern themselves.

Another point about autonomy is that it makes government at the local level continue to be worthwhile. Citizens know that the decisions taken at the local level are bound to have an impact on them in many respects, including social, cultural, economic, and environmental. Such knowledge cannot cause democratic behaviour, but it cannot hurt it, either. Citizens are more likely to participate in public life when there is a public life, as opposed to a mere bureaucratic admin-istration to which only bureaucrats belong. All other things being equal, local autonomy encourages participation in public life rather than discourages it.

The federal guarantee of autonomy at the local level also assists in the development of democracy by enhancing competitiveness throughout the system. Not to put too fine a point on it, federalism institutionalizes a system of competitive elites. There are always at least two political arenas, national and regional, and usually more. Canadian arenas also include municipal politics and Aboriginal polit-ical organizations and communities. These political arenas are not sealed off from one another. On the contrary, the politicians in one arena often scrap with those in another, sometimes on account of genuine policy disagreements, sometimes in an effort to shift the blame for problems that have developed on their watch. The beneficiaries of these engagements are the citizens, who are apt to learn more from more debate, not less debate.

Federalism, Equality, and Shared Rule

The federal principle of equality is arguably another support of democracy. Democracy presumes that individuals are political equals. This presumption is the reason individuals can agree to abide by the decision of the majority, even if they think that the decision is wrong. Since each is a political equal of the other, the weight of the majority is persuasive – the numbers rule. The decision is not a matter of who is on the winning side, as if some were superior to others. Nor is it a matter of the quality of the argument that prevails. In the end it is simply a matter of whether enough people agree on a decision.

The equality principle is a crucial principle of federalism, too, although in federalism it applies to the member units rather than to individuals. Moreover, in most federal systems equality is manifest principally in the fact that each member unit is assigned the same set of governmental responsibilities as the others. The units may well differ in such dimensions as geographic size, population size, and the size and robustness of the economy, but their governments are assigned the same tasks under the constitution.

Is equality manifest in the institutions of shared rule? There are theoretical reasons for thinking that it should be. Elazar maintains that federal systems and democracies both have roots in the biblical tradition of people making covenants with God. In the secular world people make covenants among themselves to form larger political communities. Covenanting implies equality. "Covenantal foundings," Elazar (1994, 20) writes, "emphasize the deliberate coming together of humans as equals to establish bodies politic in such a way that all reaffirm their fundamental equality and retain their basic rights."

Covenants are negotiated by equal partners who then accept to honour them. They are entered into in good faith. Precisely because they are agreements among equals they are the product of choice, not force. Agreements reached by force of arms or some other intimidating resource are treaties among unequals, like the victor and the vanquished at the conclusion of war.

In the federal system, the equality of the member units only sometimes shows up in the institutions of shared rule. The design of the institutions of the central government tells the tale. Let us recall that in the United States, the Congress is a bicameral institution. The lower house, or House of Representatives, is erected on the basis of representation by population. Thus the most populous states have the most representatives and the least populous states have the fewest representatives. By contrast, in the upper house or Senate, the states are represented equally by two senators each. This interesting situation suggests that the framers of the American constitution were prepared to work two types of political equality into the design of the Congress. In the House of Representatives, the scheme of representation reflects the notion of individual political equality. In the Senate, the scheme of representation reflects the notion of the equality of the states that formed the United States.

Australia uses the same design of representation by population in the lower house and equal state representation in the Senate, but none of the other older federal systems does. Switzerland, Canada, Germany, Austria, and India opted for unequal state representation in the upper house. In these federations, the constituent states are represented in the upper house, to be sure, but not equally. For example, in Switzerland the smallest cantons have half the representation in the Council of States as the largest cantons.

Thus far we have focused on the ways in which the equality of the member units is given effect – or not – in the institutions of shared rule. It is important to consider further whether equality is joined with election. In the federations mentioned above, the lower houses are all elective institutions. The upper houses are a different story. In the United States, the method of selection used to be indirect election, with the state legislatures choosing the senators. This was changed in 1913 to a system of direct, statewide elections of senators. Australia also combines equal state representation and direct election in the design of its Senate. India uses the method of indirect election by state legislatures. In Canada, where the provinces are unequally represented in the Senate, there is no election at all, since senators are appointed by the federal government. In Germany, which features unequal representation in the upper house, the state governments send their own elected representatives to that body.

The principle of shared rule implies the equality of the member states. As these examples show, however, in the actual organization of shared rule in federal systems, there is no guarantee of equality at all. Some systems feature equality and some do not. The same is true for election. The principle of shared rule implies election, but only in some federal systems are the institutions of shared rule elected. The equality principle of federalism, which attaches to the status of the member units, only leans in the direction of democracy.

Federalism and the Rule of Law

Federalism is often derided for its formalism and legalism. Critics point to such characteristic features of federations as the written constitution, the important role of the courts in interpreting the constitution, the carefully defined rules for making various types of decisions, and the carefully defined roles of the different levels of government. The overall effect, they say, is stultifying, not to say stupefying. Legal norms and practices and complex rules are emphasized over simple decision-making rules based on popular majorities.

It is true that federalism entails complex decision-making rules. Under the constitution of a federal system of government, the power to act is chopped up and distributed among a wide array of offices.

And if the constitution happens as well to stipulate the rights of individuals, public office-holders need to observe additional limitations, even when acting within the sphere of authority assigned to them. Moreover, the structural complexity generates further complexities in the form of multiple bureaucracies. Nevertheless, at the heart of the formalism and legalism is the principle of the rule of law. The importance of this principle to the practice of democracy cannot be overlooked and ought not to be understated.

The rule of law is not a necessary and sufficient condition of democracy, but it is a necessary condition of democracy. In the absence of the rule of law, it is hard to see how any democracy, to say nothing of modern mass democracies, could function at all. The reason is the stability, predictability, and order that the rule of law helps to maintain for the members of the society. In the words of the Supreme Court of Canada (*Reference re Secession of Quebec* [1998], 257), "The rule of law vouchsafes to the citizens and residents of the country a stable, predictable and ordered society in which to conduct their affairs. It provides a shield for individuals from arbitrary state action."

The Court went on to explain how the rule of law underpins an order in the society in specific ways. One is captured in the dictum of "a government of laws, not a government of men." However politically incorrect this phraseology, it expresses the timeless credo that there is one law for all, and that the law as duly enacted by the legislators governs the actions of governments and private individuals alike. No groups and no individuals are beyond or somehow above the application of the law. Any exemptions from the application of the law must be part of the law. A second, related way in which the rule of law anchors the society is the requirement that the exercise of public power be authorized by law. Government officials must act within the powers assigned to them, otherwise government becomes nothing more than arbitrary rule. So too are private individuals prevented from taking the law into their own hands, in the manner of vigilantes.

Thus conceived, the rule of law lays the foundation of trust on which a democracy needs to be built. On many occasions, members of democratic political communities are obliged to go along with the will of the majority, so long as the majority is collected in accordance with the rules agreed upon for that purpose. This is much easier when the background principle of the rule of law is in place, for it guarantees that the winners will not overreach themselves or act beyond their competence under the constitution. It guarantees that the winners will not use their valid powers under the constitution to trample the rights of the losers, or the rights of minorities, or the rights of individuals. At first glance the rule of law might seem to place shackles on democracy by limiting what a duly elected government can do. In fact, the rule of law enables democracy by establishing the foundation of trust on which the citizenry can accept the outcome of electoral battles.

Federalism and Democratic Complexity

This audit is focused on the Canadian federal system and the extent to which it encourages or discourages the democratic conduct of politics. Whatever the answer turns out to be, it is now clear that in theory the structure of a federal system harbours considerable scope for democratic institutions and practices. Yet complexities peculiar to federalism also affect democracy. Chief among them is the relationship between majorities and minorities, the examination of which means revisiting Dicey's terrain.

Political scientist R. Whitaker (1983, 2) articulates perfectly the federal approach to majoritarianism: "Modern federalism is an institutionalisation of the formal limitation of the national majority will as the legitimate ground for legislation." Precisely. Political communities that are defined geographically by boundaries – as opposed to being groups scattered throughout the larger society – are the baseline units of federal systems. They are interested in joining together without dissolving their particularities into a union and losing themselves in a greater whole. "They must desire union," Dicey (1893, 141) wrote, "and must not desire unity," a state of affairs that he professed to find peculiar indeed. Thus they negotiate to maintain specified areas of self-government in which local majorities prevail. This is the formal limitation on the will of the national majority to which Whitaker refers. It means, at the very least, that there are majorities within the territorially based communities that comprise the federation as well as a national majority. These majorities imply minorities, too.

If there is a national majority, there is a national minority. If there are majorities in the territorially based communities, there are minorities in them as well. So different combinations of majorities and minorities are found. This situation might not be a problem, especially wherever the population of the federation as a whole is homogeneous. Or, if not homogeneous (which is highly unlikely), then a melting pot, to use the phrase often applied (correctly or not) to American society. In the melting-pot society, no ethnic or national minority is territorially based and armed with a claim to self-rule. Political theorist Will Kymlicka (1998, 136-8) uses the phrase "territorial federalism" to describe a federation designed on the assumption that there is no territorially based national minority to accommodate. In his view, the United States is a clear example of territorial federalism since the system was not designed to accommodate the claims of particular ethnocultural groups.

What about federations that were designed, in part, to meet such claims? Kymlicka calls them examples of multination federalism, in which nationality-based units possess recognition of who they are and powers that are somewhat commensurable with their self-government claims. Belgium is one such example. Belgium contains three territorially defined regions, one of which is coextensive with the (Dutch-speaking) Flemish community and one with the (French-speaking) Walloons. The third is the Brussels Region, which houses much of the officialdom of the European Community. The polarization of the Flemish and the Walloons is one of the reasons for the country's use of the federal structure.

Kymlicka regards Canada, correctly in my view, as a territorial federalism with some multination features. Canada followed the model of American federalism in treating the Canadian provinces essentially as legal equals (irrespective of who happens to reside within them). Thus in Canada, as already noted, under the Constitution each of the provinces is assigned the same subject matters of legislation. In addition, however Quebec and the Acadian community in New Brunswick add multination features.

The province of Quebec is the home of the Québécois, the French-speaking community that is described by some as a nation or a people. The Québécois also form a majority within the province. Some would say their presence is the main reason Canada is a federation at all, since so many of the political leaders from the other colonies would have preferred the option of a legislative union. Constitutionally speaking, some account is taken of the Québécois. To mention one example, the Constitution as enacted in 1867 provides for the use of French or English in the legislatures and courts of Canada and Quebec. This provision was not applied to any other province at that time.

Such a provision does not make Canada a multination federalism, at least not in Kymlicka's sense of that concept. It does, however, illustrate the complexities of majorities and minorities where there are territorially based ethnocultural groups or nations. After all, the language provision speaks to the minority as well as the majority. In Quebec the largest language minority was and still is English-speaking, and the language provision was meant to facilitate its participation in political and legal life in the province. In Canada the largest language minority was and still is French-speaking, and the language provision was meant to facilitate its participation in these same important spheres in the national arena.

The Acadian community in New Brunswick presents a different situation from Quebec, since it is a minority French-speaking community in the province, the majority of which is anglophone. At roughly 40 percent of the province's population, however, it is a substantial minority, the members of which are concentrated in the northwest, northeast, and southeast corners of the province. In 1982 New Brunswick entered the constitutionally mandated regime of official languages, with the result that the Acadian minority gained rights in connection with the French language that are entrenched in the

Constitution. In 1993, at the behest of New Brunswick, the Constitution was amended to establish recognition of the equality of the two linguistic communities in the province (Hurley 1996, 93-6). This interesting provision extends the notion of equality beyond language to the status of the community as a whole. Even so, in strict numerical terms, the Acadian community in New Brunswick, like the much smaller one in Nova Scotia, which does not enjoy the same range of language rights, is a minority twice over – in the province and nationally.

The federal structure is not an easy solution to the problem of the peaceful coexistence of diverse nationalities in their various minority and majority formations. In addition to decisions about rights that affect minority communities, such as language rights, the dimension of symbolic politics arises in relation to the issue of "founding peoples." In Canada some describe the origins of the country in terms of two founding peoples, French and English. These founding peoples are held to be equals. Others talk about three founding peoples, English, French, and Aboriginal, again considered to be equals. The founding-peoples contention in whatever guise has become increasingly awkward to maintain, particularly in the light of the emphasis on individual rights and freedoms in the Canadian Charter of Rights and Freedoms. Moreover, many prefer instead to see the country as a multicultural construct that engages an ever changing portrait of individual citizens and their communities. The federal system fuels the always provocative claim of founding peoples at the same time as it assuages the demand of territorially based communities for recognition of their very existence.

Dicey held that federalism was undemocratic to the extent that it permitted minorities to obstruct majorities. But the phenomenon of minorities versus majorities might also be regarded as a matter of democratic complexity. There is always a need to be sensitive to the relationship between minorities and majorities, and especially when the relationship between them is intensified by the multination factor. One indication that special heed is paid to the relationship between majorities and minorities in federations is the range of decision-making rules that is utilized in them. An example is the

United States, the constitution of which stipulates the use, on various occasions, of the simple majority rule and the supermajority rule (two-thirds and three-quarters). Similarly, the Canadian Constitution provides for the simple majority rule, a supermajority rule of seven out of ten provinces or two-thirds, and unanimity. Whenever they appear, such requirements over and beyond the simple majority imply that the simple majority is not held to be enough, and that a broader consensus is needed to undergird some decisions in order for them to be given effect.

Conclusion

In his analysis of the reasons for the establishment of federations, Riker reminds us that the pursuit of democracy is not necessarily high on the list. The desire for economic expansion and the need for security from military aggression are significant factors. On the other hand, as Livingston suggests, the societies that inhabit federal systems include distinctive communities that are territorially based. Indeed, federations are the result of the aggregation of discrete communities that see the potential for maintaining a measure of self-rule in the federal structure. That potential enables the compromise between union and autonomy that the federal structure represents. As it turns out, federalism offers more than the potential for autonomy; the potential for democracy, period, is high. The federations around the world are evidence of this point.

The federal structure is no guarantee of democracy – nothing is – but certainly it encourages the democratic conduct of government and politics. As outlined in the chapter, the specific reasons for this begin with the opportunity for self-rule that federalism affords the territorially based communities that join the federation. There is also the principle of equality, which is part and parcel of both the federal system and democracy. In the federal system equality begins with the treatment of the founding units as equals, and it grows from there. In democracy, the political equality of the individual is the central assumption from which majority rule proceeds, and then equality grows from there. The emphasis on equality in federalism and in democracy is mutually reinforcing. Finally, there is the principle of the rule of law. The federal system is a formal, legal structure complete with rules that are enforceable in the courts. It is reliant upon the rule of law, without which it is inoperable. Indeed, precisely this quality of the system recommends it to the weaker of the communities that join it. They know that they can seek to have their rights under the constitution enforced in the courts. But the rule of law is also the foundation of the orderly regime within which a democratic politics is conducted. In the absence of order and predictability, democracy is not sustainable.

Despite the harmony between federalism and democracy, it is also true that federalism complicates democracy. Federalism sets up a situation in which majorities and minorities come up against one another continually, sometimes in the same shape and other times in shifting shapes. Conflict is inevitable. Managing the conflict through democratic means is an enormous challenge that requires sophisticated attitudes and instruments. The task of this audit is to determine whether the forms and formalities of Canadian federalism hinder the conduct of democracy in the country, establishing nothing more than the endless complications and obstacles that lead some to think that federalism is a drag on democratic rule. Or do these same forms and formalities capitalize on the democratic potential that is inherent in any federal structure? To this end, the next chapter lays out the specifics of Canadian federalism.

CHAPTER 2

- Each level of government has autonomous decision-making power within the areas assigned to it.
- Federalism is the alternative to empire.
- Acton saw in the structure of federalism a conservative bias.
- Executive federalism stifles the open competition among governments for the support of the citizens that classical federalism is admirably designed to promote.
- There is a reciprocity between the structure of federalism and democracy.
- Federalism offers democrats an organizational structure that is founded on the equality principle.
- Federalism institutionalizes a system of competitive elites.

CANADIAN FEDERALISM

3

The fathers of Confederation did not claim to be democrats, and few were federalists. Indeed, some of them were articulate antidemocrats, and some were openly hostile to the idea of organizing the system along federal lines. These points need to be kept in mind in reviewing the Canadian federal system from the standpoint of the democratic audit. If the handiwork of the fathers comes up short in the audit, well, it's for good reason. The record of the heirs of the fathers – our record – is another matter altogether.

Antidemocrats

Before making hay out of the antidemocratic rhetoric of the fathers of Confederation, who were, after all, nineteenth-century colonial figures, we should be clear about their views on democracy. They thought it was mob rule, which helps to explain their aversion to it. Most Canadians today are likely averse to mob rule, too, but in all probability most Canadians regard themselves as democrats. The difference is that we have a broader view of democracy than the founders of the Constitution, who defined it narrowly, to mean people acting outside of the prescribed rules and procedures, or even in violation of them.

The mob-rule view of democracy of the founders was articulated clearly by one of their number, D'Arcy McGee, the Irish immigrant then at the height of a successful political career in Quebec. McGee identified democracy, especially American democracy, with too much equality, too much liberty, and too little respect for authority. He was bothered especially by the idea of the equality of individuals. He called it an "unreal equality," and warned that it was the kind of idea that ran roughshod over things like respect for the law for its own sake (McGee 1865, 131).

Does this mean that McGee and his colleagues were opposed to elected office? Of course not. The leading voices of the Confederation project were elected politicians. But they were opposed to a government constructed upon only one principle – the rule of the many – and only one method of selection, election. They wanted to see in addition the counterprinciple of the rule of the meritorious (in some way) few, in the form of a conservatively disposed, appointed chamber that would serve to check the elected one. The founders also believed in constitutional monarchy and the monarchical principle, as it was called at the time. Canada is no longer referred to as the Dominion of Canada, but it remains a constitutional monarchy. These three elements – election, merit, and monarchy – were already interwoven in the British constitution, which they were inclined to regard as the only model worth following.

The British model that the founders admired and attempted to replicate included several important principles: the monarchical principle (the Crown), the aristocratic principle (the House of Lords), the responsibility of the government to an elected legislative body (the House of Commons), an independent judiciary, and the rule of law. The founders produced a written Constitution that incorporated as many of these principles as possible as well as the federal principle, then still a novel idea to people outside of the United States. The combination of such principles in a written constitution is often described as a constitutional system or simply constitutionalism. Following this definitional line, the founders were constitutionalists, not simple democrats. They were constitutionalists who were willing to take a chance on federalism.

Reluctant Federalists

The background events leading to Confederation in 1867 as well as the event itself have been recorded by Canadian historians, whose work need not be duplicated here. It suffices to state that the Confederation project was spearheaded by some of the political leaders of the province of Canada, which then consisted of Canada West (part of what is now Ontario) and Canada East (part of what is now Quebec). These men had a number of reasons for seeking to expand the boundaries of their community, not the least of which was the near impossibility of governing it. It was proving very difficult for governments to find the support of the majority in the elected legislature, which majority they needed in order to survive. As a result, governments were falling with alarming regularity. The successful negotiation of some type of union of the province of Canada and the other colonies of British North America — Nova Scotia, New Brunswick, Prince Edward Island, and Newfoundland — was a way of breaking the political deadlock.

Not everyone was keen on the project, including groups within and without the province. Within, some French-speaking political leaders in Canada East were concerned about the prospect of the French-speaking community becoming a permanent minority within a larger union dominated by English-speaking inhabitants. For their part, some English-speaking political leaders in Canada West thought the larger union would only complicate their relationship with the French community, and therefore preferred that the province resolve its problems on its own.

Without, union was opposed by some in the Maritime provinces who feared for the fate of the small Maritime communities in a union with the larger Canadian communities, or "central Canada," a phrase used even then. Nevertheless, when a delegation of Canadian politicians travelled to Charlottetown, PEI, in September 1864 to pitch the project to the Maritime political leaders, they generated enough interest in the idea to justify holding another meeting a month later in Quebec City. There the delegates of the colonies hammered out the Quebec Resolutions. Although modifications were made to the resolutions at a conference hosted by the British government in London in 1866, in essence they were unchanged (Canada 1961, Annex 4, 66-76). As such, they remain a cornerstone of the Canadian Constitution, and can be found in the Constitution Act, 1867.

There is irony in the fact that the delegates established a federal system. In the British North American colonies, the conventional wisdom of the day favoured the British unitary model, or legislative union, as it was called. The Canadian leader, John A. Macdonald, called it "the best, the cheapest, the most vigorous, and the strongest system of government we could adopt" (Waite 1963, 40). Nevertheless it was pretty widely understood that a legislative union of the colonies was not in the cards, largely because the French-speaking and Maritime communities simply would not accept it. Therefore the delegates attending the Quebec conference opted for the only alternative that met their concerns, the federal model. For many of them federalism meant a venture into the unknown.

However normal federalism might appear to Canadians today, it was anything but in 1864. To start, there was no widely accepted public view of the meaning of the "federal principle," as it was called at the time. Some thought that it meant a division of powers between the central and local governments. Others thought that it described the composition of the central legislature, in particular the balance between the House of Commons and the Senate. Still others held that it was not possible to marry federalism and the British parliamentary system. Commenting on the debate on the proposed Quebec Resolutions that took place throughout the colonies, the historian

Peter Waite writes that "when analysis of the federal principle was attempted, many newspapers, and not a few politicians, simply bogged down" (Waite 1963, 112).

Moreover, the only model of federalism was the American one right next door – and it was not terribly popular. At the time the Canadians were embarking on the Confederation project, the Americans were fighting a civil war. The federal system, or at least the American version, was suspected to be a contributing factor. Macdonald argued that the design flaw in the US federal system was to specify the powers of the Congress and then to leave the rest, or the residual power, to the states. To his mind, the possession by the states of the residual power signified state sovereignty, and the idea of state sovereignty spelled trouble. The reason was that local authorities, secure in the local attachments of the people, might well seek to aggrandize power. Macdonald was convinced that local authorities would win in any contest between themselves and the national authorities. Accordingly, he urged the delegates to correct the American error by specifying the powers of the local legislature as well as the powers of the central legislature, and then assigning the residual power to the central legislature (Browne 1969, 122). This the delegates did.

In reviewing the key federal features of the Constitution, it is helpful to keep in mind the effort of the Quebec delegates to accommodate the desire for local self-government of the small Maritime communities and the larger French-speaking community and at the same time to establish the strong central government characteristic of a legislative union like Britain. In a sense the delegates were trying to do two different things at once, an effort captured by the phrase then in use, "federal union." In theory the phrase is an oxymoron because it implies two contradictory things at the same time. Yet in fact it accurately describes the Constitution that the delegates produced, which mixes features from the federal model and the union model.

Leading Features of Canadian Federalism

CENTRAL GOVERNMENT: HOUSE OF COMMONS

The delegates to the Quebec conference were parliamentarians. They were political leaders in the British colonies that had acquired the system of responsible government, in Nova Scotia early in 1848 and in the rest of the colonies shortly thereafter. As everyone knows, under this system, the government must retain the support of a majority of the elected legislature. Further, again following the British model, the colonial legislatures were bicameral or two-house affairs, with an elected lower house and an appointed upper house. The delegates were certain to retain the parliamentary system that they knew so well in the new national government. At issue was the extent to which they would choose to modify it in accordance with federal considerations. This issue arose immediately with the House of Commons.

The delegates agreed that the democratic principle of representation by population – "rep by pop" – would govern the distribution of seats in the elected House. Under it, the seats are assigned to each province (and now territories, too) in proportion with its population. The principle is simple enough. But the PEI delegates were disgruntled to discover that it yielded the Island a mere five seats out of the initial number of 194. "Only five members out of 194," argued Island delegate T.H. Haviland, "would give the Island no position" (Browne 1969, 108). The Island's attorney general, Edward Palmer, complained that rep by pop was "not applicable" to a union in which the provinces were asked to surrender "their own self-government and individuality" (Browne 1969, 108). A practical problem arose too because PEI consisted then (and still does) of three counties among which it was deemed impossible to distribute five seats. There was also the sensitive division between Catholics and Protestants. Accordingly, PEI battled for an even six.

The issue caused quite a wrangle at the Quebec conference. One of the staunchest advocates of rep by pop was George Brown, leader of the Reform party in Canada West. Rep by pop was a touchy issue in the province of Canada. At its establishment in 1841, Canada West and Canada East had been assigned the same number of seats in the province's legislature, even though the eastern half had a larger population than the western half. Of course this underrepresentation of Canada East was deliberate, being a key element of the British government's plan to assimilate the French to the anglophone world. The assimilation project was a complete failure. But when the demographic tables turned, and the population of Canada West began to outstrip Canada East's, then leaders like Brown unashamedly began the cry for rep by pop – although to no immediate avail. When Brown joined Macdonald to advance the federal scheme, it was on the condition that the factor of population drive the distribution of seats in the new House of Commons. Thus he was exasperated by the position of the Island delegates at the conference, as indicated in this response that he made to them:

> To give Prince Edward Island five members the total properly
> should be 205. It is obvious we cannot depart from representa-
> tion by population. The only thing to do would be to take Prince
> Edward Island as the basis which would give a House of 230,
> altogether too large. Give one member to each county and let
> the whole Island elect the other two, and keep the number five
> intact; or let the whole Island elect five. We should have to add
> thirty-eight members to the house in order to give Prince Edward
> Island six, as the basis of representation by population (Browne
> 1969, 111).

In the end, the Islanders were overridden on the issue. Samuel Leonard Tilley, premier of New Brunswick, found their opposition to a strict population formula "singular," and reminded the delegates that "it was fully understood at Charlottetown that those who came to the Conference expected representation by population" (Browne 1969, 108). Tilley's position was typical of the Maritime delegates at the conference, and Maritime pro-unionists (as supporters of Confederation were often called) generally. Even an avowed anti-Confederate pamphleteer like Martin Wilkins (1867, 20) of Nova Scotia conceded the "justness of representation by population in the Lower Branch." He simply thought it was a mistake for the small Maritime provinces to join a federation in which they stood to be overwhelmed by the large Canadian provinces in the House of Commons. So did Joseph Howe, Nova Scotia's leading anti-Confederate, and his analysis was razor sharp.

Howe argued that under the Quebec scheme, the centre of power and influence would always remain in Canada because there were no countervailing forces to offset it. He drew a contrast between the House of Commons and the US House of Representatives. In the American body, he argued, the smaller states were somewhat protected by the higher number of large states. These balanced and controlled each other so that no one state could dominate the rest. Under the Quebec scheme, however, the two sections of Canada could be expected to combine against the lower provinces whenever their interests clashed with those of the latter, and the lower provinces would have no other large provinces to lean on for protection. Moreover, the Maritime provinces themselves were not united. If Maritime union had been permitted prior to Confederation, Howe thought, they might have had a chance to organize and protect themselves, "but, disunited, it is plain that they must be prey to the spoiler; and having but forty-seven representatives, all told, it is apparent that the Government of the confederacy will always rest upon the overwhelming majority of 147, and that, even when close divisions and ministerial crises occur, the minority can easily be split up and played off against each other for purely Canadian purposes" (Howe 1909, 490).

Howe articulated forcefully and clearly what was at stake in the issue of representation in the House of Commons. Notwithstanding the power of his argument, Nova Scotia entered Confederation at the start, while PEI declined to join until 1873. Since then, the small provinces have fought against their demographic fate in terms of declining seat shares in the House, not without some success. In 1915 the Constitution was amended at the behest of the Maritime provinces to provide that no province have fewer seats (and therefore members of Parliament) than senators. Today the "senatorial floor" amendment protects the number of seats assigned to PEI, New Brunswick, and Newfoundland and Labrador. Without it, these provinces would be entitled to fewer seats in the House than they have now. Moreover, the oft-contested formula that is used to convert the constitutional principles of representation into the assignment of seats also contains some protection for the least populous provinces (Courtney 2001, 23-7).

Clearly there is nothing simple about a democratic audit of federalism. Democratic and federal claims can intersect and clash. In the House, the more populous provinces have always had too few seats in relation to the less populous provinces and are not wildly enthusiastic about it. The less populous provinces have always had too many seats in relation to the larger ones and still think they are poorly served. The large provinces press the democratic principle and the small provinces press the federal principle. They do so within a horizon of self-interest, analyzing the likely effect of the representation formula on their respective political interests. This is as true of the Senate as it is of the House.

CENTRAL GOVERNMENT: SENATE

From the point of view of the Maritime provinces, the design of the Senate is something of a mystery. It is hard not to think that the Maritime delegates were asleep at the switch. To some extent they laboured under the spell of the parliamentary institutions that they knew so well. This explains their inclination to view the upper house more as a parliamentary institution like the House of Lords than a federal one like the American Senate. Still, the composition of the Senate was the subject of some argument among the delegates, and was the first specific question they addressed at the Quebec conference.

Macdonald moved that the provinces be organized in three sections, each section possessing equal representation, the trick being that Ontario and Quebec would constitute two sections and the four

Atlantic provinces the third section. The records of the debate that followed are sketchy, but they do indicate Maritime objections. The Maritime delegates were prepared to accept the idea of equal regional representation over equal provincial representation, and they agreed to the figure of twenty-four members per section. But they demanded better numbers on the third section and got them. Newfoundland was dropped from it, and instead assigned four members of its own. That left a three-province section, set at ten members each for New Brunswick and Nova Scotia, and four for PEI, which seemed settled until PEI discovered that George Brown's formula for representation in the House of Commons assigned it only five seats there. As detailed above, it wanted six, and the paltry five made the Senate four increasingly unacceptable. And so PEI lobbied – in vain – for an additional seat in the House rather than in the Senate.

Only the Island delegate A.A. Macdonald made the case for equal provincial representation in the Senate, citing the US Senate as a desirable model. He urged that equal provincial representation was the appropriate quid pro quo for the population-driven membership of the lower house. Then he made the argument that the small provinces were the constitutional equals of the large provinces and therefore were entitled to equal representation in a body that was supposed to guard provincial rights and privileges (Browne 1969, 138). Nevertheless, the delegates rejected the idea of equal provincial representation in the Senate, not regarding the American example as a compelling one.

On the hustings, however, it was a different matter, and anti-Confederates made liberal use of the American example. To say that they were really worried by the design of the proposed Senate is an understatement. For example, in New Brunswick premier A.J. Smith had been defeated by Tilley's pro-union party in a second election over the Confederation issue. Faced with the new government's resolution authorizing delegates to attend a conference in London, England, later in the year to finalize the details of the Quebec scheme, Smith vainly drew attention to its defects, especially the upper house. Arguing that it left the provinces with no effective check in the central government, he suggested that this was a more serious problem here than in the United States, since the "popular branch in that country could not make and unmake Administrations as the Commons of the Confederation can." For that very reason, he continued, "little New Brunswick" deserved much greater representation in the upper house than it was assigned to compensate for its insufficient numbers in the lower house: "Give us, at least, the guard which they have in the United States, although we ought to have more, because, here, the popular branch is all-powerful" (Smith 1866, 1).

If the composition of the Senate favoured the larger provinces, then the large-province spokesmen were not about to press the point. Indeed, they were hardly interested in the Senate as a federal body at all. Macdonald made a vague statement or two about the protection of sectional interests, but his real concern was to defend the Crown appointment of senators, which, as everyone knew, meant appointment by the government of the day. Voters in the province of Canada had been accustomed to electing legislative councillors since 1856, so the reversion to appointment was bound to be a disappointment to the more democratically minded among them and needed defending. For his part, Brown had little to say about the Senate as a federal upper house. For him it was a concession to "French Canadian interests" in return for Canada West's just desserts (representation by population) in the House of Commons.

For those who suspected that the Senate was a federal fraud, Christopher Dunkin's argument must have been conclusive. Dunkin, Liberal representative of Brome in the Eastern Townships, declared it the "merest sham," with nothing of the federal principle about it. Since his model for purposes of evaluation was the US Senate, he had an easy time making the case. His conclusion, which is really too good to pass over, was that while the Canadian Senate, with its absolute veto, might prove a "first-rate deadlock" mechanism, it could not be a "federal check." Possessing no real power except the negative one of the veto, and representing no public opinion, let alone opinion in the provinces, the Senate, he declaimed, was "a very near approach to the worst system which could be devised in legislation" (Province of Canada 1865, 494-5).

It can be concluded that from the point of view of the small provinces, the Senate was a lost opportunity. For the large provinces, on the other hand, it was something of a victory for precisely that reason. Given its design, the Senate would never be able to counter the weight of the large provinces in the House of Commons. Still, it could not be expected that the political interests of the provinces qua provinces would find no representation in the capital. They would have to find a home, and if not in the Senate, then somewhere else. According to Dunkin, the default option was the cabinet:

> I have to ask honorable gentlemen opposite how they are going to organize their Cabinet, for these provinces, according to this so called Federal scheme? (Hear, hear.) I think I may defy them to shew that the Cabinet can be formed on any other principle than that of a representation of the several provinces in that Cabinet. It is admitted that the provinces are not really represented to any Federal intent in the Legislative Council. The cabinet here must discharge all that kind of function, which in the United States is performed, in the Federal sense, by the Senate (Province of Canada 1865, 495).

When all is said and done, then, the PEI delegates were not asleep at the switch – they exercised good judgment in choosing to fight for an extra Commons seat rather than more Senate seats.

CENTRAL GOVERNMENT: CABINET

By comparison with the huge volume of argumentation on the House of Commons and the Senate, the references to that really key parliamentary institution, the cabinet, were scant. Critics of Confederation had the most to say. Proponents of the scheme said next to nothing, an exception being George-Étienne Cartier, a leading figure from Canada East in the coalition government. In a series of interjections in the midst of Dunkin's comments on the cabinet, Cartier made it quite clear that he was fully alive to the importance for the French-

speaking community of representation there and that he was prepared to see that they got it (Province of Canada 1865, 498-500).
Maritime anti-Confederates could see the need for representation in
the cabinet, too. But first it is useful to explore further Dunkin's pre-
scient reasoning on the federal role of the cabinet.

Dunkin thought that in the context of a federation, the traditional
parliamentary cabinet was an awkward fit. "How are we to make it
[the cabinet] work," he asked, "engrafted on a system which, in its
essentials, is after all more American than British?" And he answered
that it could be made to work only on the basis of provincial representation. The cabinet would be unable to escape the political pressures of a union constructed on federal lines. Since the provinces
were not represented "to any Federal intent" in the Senate, which had
no executive powers anyway, they had to be present in the true executive, the cabinet, "whenever a Federal check is needed." Thus the
Canadian cabinet would be forced to substitute for the lack of a gen-
uinely federal upper house:

> And precisely as in the United States, whenever a Federal check
> is needed, the Senate has to do Federal duty as an integral part of
> the Executive Government. So here, when that check cannot be
> so got, we must seek such substitute for it as we may, in a Federal
> composition of the Executive Council [cabinet]; that is to say, by
> making it distinctly representative of the provinces (Province of
> Canada 1865, 497).

The idea of the cabinet doing federal duty was ominous for the
small provinces. The House of Commons generates the cabinet.
Therefore their slight representation in the Commons would count
against the small provinces twice, once in the House, and again in the
cabinet. The reverse was true for the large provinces. And large
provinces had something else going for them in terms of cabinet for-
mation, an intangible but nonetheless important opinion extant that
cabinets in parliamentary systems ought to be constructed on the
basis of competence and experience. Dunkin expressed this view

when, having concluded that the cabinet would become a federal body, he added disapprovingly that this was entirely inconsistent with British constitutional practice, which contemplated a cabinet working as "one unit," a national body concerned with the interests of the nation as a whole, not a body of "sections" (Canada 1865, 497).

Joseph Howe saw the problem of the cabinet for the small provinces with utter clarity. On a number of occasions, he referred contemptuously to the probability of "Canadian" dominated ministries resting securely on the "permanent parliamentary majority" vouchsafed to the Canadas by virtue of their comparatively large populations. Howe understood fully the role of the cabinet in the responsible-government model, as he had been the principal author of the model in Nova Scotia. Therefore he forecast dire consequences of a Canadian-dominated cabinet for the Maritime provinces. Prominent among these was foregone patronage, as well as economic problems having to do with the loss of control of public policy on such issues as free trade versus protectionism and tax policy. Nevertheless, his great concern was patronage, and he held a deep appreciation of the cabinet's role in it. By patronage, he meant contracts and jobs as well as appointments, but here he is on the cabinet's powers of appointment: "Mr. Brown or Mr. Galt may select for governor, or councillor, or collector, the most obnoxious, profligate, or distasteful person in either province [New Brunswick or Nova Scotia], and there is no revision or redress. Secure of the support of his Canadian majority he may laugh at our complaints, and regard even our criticism as an impertinence" (Howe 1909, 491). In the opening line of the very first article of *The Botheration Scheme* – a series of twelve newspaper articles penned against the proposed Constitution – Howe had warned against handing the patronage and revenues of Nova Scotia to the Canadians. "Before deciding to hand over to the Canadians the patronage and revenues of Nova Scotia," he stated flatly, "let us enquire whether there is anything in our present condition to compel us to make this transfer" (Howe 1865, 1).

Contemporary political-science opinion completely vindicates the assessments of Dunkin and Howe. Political scientist John Courtney

(2001, 33) states that the cabinet is the country's "principal federal representational institution." It is essential for the provinces to gain representation there for a number of reasons, chief among them economic reasons. Political scientist Herman Bakvis (1991, 299) explains: "For the majority of provinces, including all four in the Atlantic region that depend upon Ottawa for close to half their revenues, the success in extracting funding beyond the basic transfer payments is in part based on the presence of strong representation in cabinet."

RATIFICATION OF THE CONSTITUTION

Ratification is an important feature of the constitutional process, a feature that can be evaluated by democratic and federal standards. Was the proposed constitution voted by the people? Was the proposed constitution voted by the people in each of the communities fated to enter the federation? These standards are hard to apply to the Canadian case, however, because the ratification process itself was so dubious. Indeed, "ratification" is probably the wrong word if it is meant to imply popular consent. What can be stated with complete accuracy is that the standards set in the ratification of the US constitution were not met here. The Americans established, first, election in the form of state conventions elected for the purpose of voting on the proposed constitution; and second, unanimity in the requirement that only states that had ratified the document could join the union. One of the framers of the American constitution, James Madison (1977, 274), described the significance of the process: "Each state, in ratifying the Constitution, is considered as a sovereign body, independent of all others, and only to be bound by its own voluntary act."

British colonialism put paid to the idea that sovereign states could be involved in ratifying the Quebec resolutions. The provinces were colonies and the British Parliament had to agree to any new constitutional scheme involving them. Ratification therefore boiled down to the consent required in the colonies before they could request the British Parliament to act. The delegates at the Quebec conference

decided that a favourable vote on the resolutions in the colonial legislatures was sufficient for the purpose, no amendments permitted.
But they did not even manage to get that consent – not really.

In the province of Canada, the coalition government that had initiated and pursued the Confederation agreement successfully
marched it through the legislature. A relatively substantial debate
took place on the agreement, although the vote in favour of it was a
foregone conclusion. The small provinces, by contrast, demurred. In
Prince Edward Island the legislature voted it down. In Nova Scotia
and New Brunswick the best that the governments could do was to
get their respective legislatures to support a resolution to send delegates to London to confer with the Canadians and the British on a
constitutional scheme. Which scheme was not clear. What is clear is
that the Quebec resolutions themselves were never agreed to by
either legislature. Moreover, the issue was never returned to the legislatures. At the London conference held in December 1866, and
attended by British officials and delegates from Canada, New Brunswick, and Nova Scotia – PEI and Newfoundland having dropped out –
some minor changes were made to the Quebec resolutions, and the
result was transformed into the Bill for the Confederation of British
North America that was passed by the British Parliament the following spring. The process was expeditious, but not especially democratic or federal.

DIVISION OF POWERS

Thus far the federal features of the national government and the
process of ratifying the Constitution have been examined. None
incorporates the federal principle of the equality of the member
states. One crucial feature does, however: namely the distribution of
subject matters or jurisdictions between Parliament and the provincial legislatures.

Assigning the power to legislate in specified areas to different levels of government is a quintessentially federal idea. But there are different ways of doing it. For instance, as noted earlier in the chapter,

the Americans chose to assign a list of subjects to the Congress, and left whatever subjects remained to the states. The Quebec delegates chose instead to list the subjects assigned to Parliament, and then the subjects assigned to the provincial legislatures. They added a third, small list of subjects on which both might legislate, stipulating that in the event of a conflict of laws, Parliament would prevail. They rounded off the scheme by assigning to Parliament a general power to legislate for the peace, order, and good government of Canada. This "peace, order and good government" clause – or pogg, as it is dubbed by students of the Constitution – immediately precedes the list of subjects assigned to Parliament.

Some important points about the distribution of powers need to be stressed. One is that each province possesses the same set of subject areas on which to legislate. In this respect, the equality of the member states is given effect. Another is that these provincial subject areas are exclusive. In other words, when legislating within them, the provincial legislatures are sovereign, or independent of Parliament. Parliament's subject areas are exclusive to it, too. In legal parlance, Parliament and the provincial legislatures possess independent spheres of jurisdiction. That having been said, two caveats must be entered here. The Constitution gives the federal government the powers of disallowance and reservation, thereby enabling it to disallow a provincial bill within a year of its passage, or to have a provincial bill reserved (not passed) in order to consider whether it should be disallowed. These provisions prompted the Australian scholar of federalism K.C. Wheare (1963, 19) to comment that Canada is "quasi-federal." These two powers, while in theory carrying enormous legal significance, have fallen into disuse, and some argue that they ought to be dropped from the Constitution as relics of a bygone era.

Two other constitutional twists need to be mentioned as well. One is that the list of subject matters assigned to Parliament includes "Indians, and Lands reserved for the Indians." Parliament alone was given the authority to legislate in relation to these peoples who, it must be said, were treated in effect as a legislative category. The second is an item in the provincial list which reads "Municipal Institutions in the Province." In other words, the municipalities and cities of the provinces are subject to the legislative jurisdiction of the provincial legislatures. They are not independent government institutions.

This completes the list of the federal features of the Canadian Constitution as established in 1867. Compared with the definition of federalism offered in Chapter 2, it comes up short. Canadian federalism was incomplete. The Quebec delegates had incorporated the idea of divided government, neither level of government being subordinate to the other; the idea of the equality of the provinces, as expressed in the fact of each province possessing the same jurisdiction to legislate; and the written Constitution. Nevertheless, they had passed over the requirement of a high court empowered to review disputes between the two levels of government, a constitutional amending formula designed to prevent any one government of the federation from acting unilaterally to change the Constitution, and a central government institution unequivocally designed to represent the provinces. The high court was made an option, not a requirement, there was no amending formula for the Constitution, and the Senate does not meet the test for provincial representation. Two developments since 1867, the high court and the amending formula, have brought the Canadian federal system more into line with the contemporary definition of federalism. Both are considered below. The high court and the amending formula are standard features of federal systems everywhere, but the first ministers' conference, so important to the conduct of federal-provincial-territorial relations, is unique. The Charter of Rights and Freedoms is also a uniquely Canadian document, with important implications for federalism. Thus, these two features are considered as well.

Supreme Court of Canada

At the Quebec conference, some of the delegates spoke to the idea of a high court authorized to serve as the final arbiter of federal-provincial conflict over jurisdiction, following the model of the US Supreme Court. No developed debate about the issue is on record, however, and in the end the delegates were content to assign to Parliament the power to establish a general court of appeals, whenever it chose to do so. The issue was complicated by the fact that like the colonies joining to form it, the new country would remain a colony of the British Empire and the Empire already had a high court to hear appeals from the colonies, the Judicial Committee of the Privy Council.

In the event, Parliament established the Supreme Court of Canada in 1875. Although this was a scant eight years after Confederation, the lively debate on the Court bill indicated a full appreciation of the likely role of the Court in settling disputes between the two levels of government under the Constitution. Some feared that this role would place the Court above Parliament, since the only way to undo a decision of the Court on the meaning of the Constitution is to amend the Constitution, something that Parliament alone could not do then and cannot do now. The Court turned out to have a full appreciation of its vital role as well. In its first reported constitutional decision in *Severn* v. *The Queen* (1878), the Court showed no hesitation in finding an Ontario licensing statute invalid on the ground that it invaded Parliament's jurisdiction over trade and commerce (Smith 1983, 130-1).

In 1949 appeals from the Canadian courts to the Judicial Committee were abolished with the result that the Supreme Court of Canada became the country's highest appellate court. Given the Court's sensitive role as the final arbiter of disputes arising under the Constitution – including disputes between the governments – it is important to know that the judges are appointed by the federal government alone. They hold office until the age of seventy-five.

THE AMENDING FORMULA

In some federal systems, the formulas used to amend the constitution flow from the principle of the equality of the member states, the leading examples being the United States, Switzerland, and Australia. In Germany, on the other hand, the formula is designed to reflect a hierarchy of the member states in terms of their different population sizes. Canada makes for a fascinating comparison because the formula used cuts both ways, featuring an equality of the states for some types of amendment and a hierarchy of them for others.

The Canadian amendment story is a tale of decades of caution. The Confederation agreement did not include an amending formula, an omission that exercised Nova Scotia anti-Confederates but few others. Therefore the power to amend the Constitution rested with the British Parliament, and what came to matter in Canada was the extent of agreement that was required among the governments before a bona fide request could be made to the British. (Naturally Parliament's consent was always a requirement.) A variety of conventional practices developed to cover the different elements of the process, some more settled than others. The outstanding convention in dispute was the extent of provincial consent needed for an amendment affecting the provinces. Did all of the provinces need to agree? Or a substantial number? Or a mere majority? And was Quebec's consent a necessary condition? These questions took on real urgency in 1980-1 in the bitter debate surrounding the amendments to the constitution proposed by the federal government at that time. Several other provinces joined Quebec in opposition to the federal initiative, and together they pressed the courts to clarify the need for provincial consent to amendments affecting the provinces. In 1981 the Supreme Court of Canada said that the answer was a substantial number. Quebec, unhappy with this response and now isolated in its opposition to the federal amendment initiative, went back to court to argue that the substantial number must include Quebec. In 1982 the Supreme Court said no.

On the heels of the court's 1981 decision the federal government and nine provincial governments, excluding the government of Quebec, reached agreement on the terms of the amending formula that is now entrenched in the Constitution. This surely ranks as one of the most complicated amending formulas in existence. For one thing, it is a series of formulas. Mercifully the two most important, the general formula and the unanimity formula, are straightforward enough. Under the general formula the agreement of Parliament and the legislatures of two-thirds of the provinces (i.e., seven of the current ten) that together contain 50 percent of the population of the provinces is required to amend important provisions of the Constitution that range from the Charter of Rights and Freedoms to the division of powers between Parliament and the provincial legislatures. Under the unanimity formula, Parliament and all of the provincial legislatures must agree to amendments to a specified set of items, namely, the role of the Crown, the senatorial floor rule discussed earlier, official language provisions that have national application, the composition of the Supreme Court of Canada, and the amending formula itself.

Judged by the standard of the equality of the member states of the federation, the unanimity formula is perfect. Under it little PEI, in law at least, has as much say as Ontario. The unanimity formula and the fact that each province possesses the same jurisdictional responsibilities together form the two features of the Constitution in which the equality of the provinces is given effect.

CANADIAN CHARTER OF RIGHTS AND FREEDOMS

The drama surrounding the amending formula was bound up with the proposal that a bill of rights be added to the Constitution, both being part of a constitutional-reform process that picked up steam during the 1960s and was eventually completed with the passage of the Constitution Act, 1982. This act, an addition to the existing constitutional documents, contains the Canadian Charter of Rights and Freedoms as well as the amending formula and some other items, notably a section on the rights of the Aboriginal peoples of Canada.

The Charter guarantees rights and freedoms that include such traditional rights as the freedom of conscience and religion and the right to vote; broadly stated equality rights; rights in relation to the use of the official languages, French and English; and education rights of official-language minorities. The Charter is applicable to governments, meaning federal and provincial laws and regulations and the actions of the federal and provincial governments. Anyone in Canada who thinks that his or her rights and freedoms have been infringed can go to court to seek a remedy for the infringement.

One of the notable features of the Charter is the so-called notwithstanding clause with which it concludes. Under this clause, Parliament and the provincial legislatures can shield a law from attack in the courts by those who allege that it violates specified rights and freedoms in the Charter (fundamental freedoms, equality rights, and legal rights). The shield is good for five years, after which it evaporates, unless the enacting legislature chooses to reinstate it. The reason to mention this clause in a text on federalism is its origins. The federal and provincial governments had reached a stalemate in the negotiations on a constitutional-reform package. The notwithstanding clause helped to break the stalemate because it made the proposed Charter more palatable to the provincial premiers, many of whom saw in the Charter a thinly disguised centralization device (Manfredi 2001, 181). In the end, all of the provincial premiers except the Quebec premier signed on to the package.

The Charter is deeply implicated in the politics of Canadian federalism. The proof is the country's experience under the notwithstanding clause, which has only been used three times. The third time was sensational. In December 1988 the Quebec National Assembly invoked the clause to shield its law on the use of French and English on commercial signs from attack in the courts on the ground that the law violated the free speech guarantee of the Charter. At any time this action would have provoked a storm of controversy, the politics of language being what they are. But the timing happened to coincide with a delicate phase in the progress of the proposed constitutional amendment known as the Meech Lake Accord. The accord was aimed at reconciling Quebec with the Constitution Act, 1982, which it still formally opposed. To this end, it contained a provision to recognize Quebec as a "distinct society." But the accord became increasingly unpopular with those who saw in the distinct-society provision a veiled attack on the Charter of Rights and Freedoms. The widely held view is that the Quebec government's use of the notwithstanding clause was the proverbial straw that broke the back of the accord, which was never ratified (Manfredi 2001, 186).

Beyond the notwithstanding clause, students of the Charter disagree about its general impact on the role of the provinces in the federal system. Some argue that the Charter has diminished the autonomy of the provinces because it has enabled the federally appointed judiciary to impose a new set of constraints on the kinds of public policies that provinces can pursue (Morton and Knopff 2000, 61-3); and that it has a centralizing or homogenizing effect generally on public policy. An example to illustrate the argument is the controversy about so-called third-party spending in election campaigns. The phrase "third party" refers to individuals and groups who are not candidates or political parties, and the controversy is whether they can spend money to advance the prospects of their preferred candidates or parties when the spending of the candidates and the parties themselves is limited by law. The Quebec government used to prohibit third-party spending altogether, but over the years litigation in the courts has compelled it to allow such spending (Smith and Bakvis 2002). The results of the litigation, of course, are applicable to the policies of all of the provinces as well as the federal government, hence the centralizing effect many fear.

Those who dismiss this argument point out that the Charter-based decisions of the courts apply as much to the federal government as the provinces, and so any diminution of power is felt equally at both levels. They also invoke the principle of judicial independence to counter any allegation of a federal bias on the part of a federally appointed judiciary. This is not the place to judge the controversy about the effect of the Charter on the role of the provinces in Canadian federalism. The important point to appreciate is that the Charter is part and parcel of Canadian federalism.

First Ministers' Conferences

The first ministers are the prime minister and the provincial pre-miers, the chief executives of the federal system. The First Ministers' Conference (FMC) is referred to as an extraconstitutional develop-ment because it has grown up outside of the Constitution (Smith 2002). Although not required by the Constitution and with an infor-mal and somewhat unpredictable character, first ministers' confer-ences are nevertheless a significant part of Canadian federalism. They are also a window on the state of federal-provincial relations.

The first such conference was initiated by the federal government in 1906 to discuss federal-provincial financial relations, and further conferences were held intermittently up to the Second World War, after which they were held much more frequently and were organized more elaborately. Their agendas covered a broad range of matters, from policy issues of the day to financial concerns to disagreements about the meaning of the Constitution. Often they were held at criti-cal times in the nation's history, when important new directions in public policy and in the Constitution were under consideration. The conferences have not been routinely successful; sometimes they have failed to generate the unanimous agreement of the principals on the matter before them. To date the most spectacular example of this occurred in 1981 when the Quebec premier found himself isolated from the other premiers and the prime minister on the issue of con-stitutional change and withdrew from the conference, unable to agree on the constitutional package that the others were prepared to support.

By 1990 FMCs were common enough to lead observers to regard them as a fixture of the system. Since 1990, however, there have been no formal, full-fledged FMCs but instead informal meetings called first ministers' meetings. This simply underscores the point that FMCs, no matter how important for the management of federal-provincial relations over the years, are not a requirement under the Constitution. They happen if and when they are thought to be needed by the principals, in particular the prime minister. Moreover, the FMCs have no permanently staffed operation. Few fixed rules and procedures appear to be followed at the meetings, although the prime minister always serves as the chair and the premiers speak in the order of the entry of the provinces into Confederation, at least when they are making initial formal presentations before the television cameras. Frank discussions tend to take place out of the public eye.

A related development, again extraconstitutional, is the Annual Premiers' Conference (APC), which brings together the leaders of the provincial and territorial governments. The APC has an even longer history than the FMCs, dating back to the first interprovincial conference in 1887, hosted by the premier of Quebec. In the years that followed interprovincial conferences were held sporadically. Then in 1960, again on the initiative of a Quebec premier, the idea of an annual conference was launched and since then there has been at least one a year. At these conferences the premiers — and since 1982 the territorial leaders in attendance as observers — generally exchange information on the issues under consideration and sometimes try to develop common positions amongst themselves from which to deal with the federal government. The APC is a relatively organized affair. It benefits from the assistance of a permanent secretariat and the meetings are planned well in advance.

Finally, there are two relatively recent arrivals on the scene, the Western Premiers' Conference and the Council of Atlantic Premiers. The idea of these encounters is to promote regional understanding and to develop among the political leaders a common position on issues regarded as important for their region.

Conclusion

Such are the federal features of the Canadian system. In large part, the federal design of the system was set at Confederation and has not changed fundamentally since then. The key legal developments since 1867 are the establishment of the Supreme Court of Canada, the Charter of Rights and Freedoms, and the amending formula for the

Constitution, and nothing about them departs significantly from the overall spirit of the federal system as initially established. The same can be said about the extraconstitutional developments critical to the conduct of intergovernmental relations in the federation, namely the conferences of the political leaders of the federal, provincial, and territorial governments.

Canadian federalism is unique. The features just canvassed show that it has never had a robustly democratic bent. The democratic audit that follows in the next three chapters will make that point abundantly clear.

CHAPTER 3

- The fathers of Confederation were constitutionalists who were willing to take a chance on federalism.

- Macdonald was convinced that local authorities would win in any contest between themselves and the national authorities.

- From the point of view of the small provinces, the Senate was a lost opportunity.

- First ministers' conferences, having grown up outside the Constitution, are extraconstitutional.

4 DEMOCRATIC AUDIT OF INCLUSIVENESS IN THE FEDERAL SYSTEM

By definition a democratic system of government organized along federal lines might be supposed to be more participatory, inclusive, and responsive than systems that are not federal. The reason seems simple enough: a federal system has more governments. And if there are more governments, then there must be more opportunities for citizens to participate in the decision-making processes, and more governmental capacity to respond to public concerns. But of course few things are that simple.

Federalism organizes people out of the system as well as organizing them into it. To repeat, federal systems are territorially based. Advances in high-speed communications and information technology have not changed the fact that the communities that are defined by a federal system and assigned governments with independent responsibilities are territorially based communities. These are the communities that matter the most politically. Other kinds of communities, which are not based on territory but instead rooted in dimensions like ethnicity or gender, are not part of the formal structure of federal institutions.

Further, even when the focus is restricted to territorial communities, it is clear that not all of them are part of the formal structure of federal institutions. A good example is the city. Of course cities have

governments. No matter what their size, however, cities are municipal institutions. And from the standpoint of the Constitution, municipal institutions are subjects that are assigned to the care of the
provinces. They are the legislative responsibility of the provincial
legislatures. As a result, the provinces can establish cities, disestab-
lish them, reorganize them, and decide what they do. Moreover, precisely because of their status as creatures of the provinces, the cities
as units in their own right are not represented in the institutions of
the central government.

This chapter of the democratic audit is focused on inclusion in the
institutions of the federal government. It explores the theme of who
is organized into the system and who is organized out of it. It identifies the territorial units that are formally included in the institutions
reviewed in the preceding chapter, and the weight that is given to
each of the units. In addition it identifies the communities that are
not formally included in the system. The factor of inclusion must be
sorted out first since it directly affects both participation and responsiveness. It is impossible to participate without being included; and
it is impossible to get the system to respond without participating in
it. Those who are entitled under the Constitution to be included in the
governing institutions can participate to make the institutions
responsive to their demands. Thus the audit of inclusiveness lays the
groundwork for the audits of participation and responsiveness in the
chapters that follow.

Who's In: Provincial Representation in National Governing Institutions

In Canada the provinces – as provinces – are not directly represented in the Senate or in any of the institutions of the central government. And yet there is an irony lurking here because Canadian federalism certainly looks to be province-based. Every single one of the
institutions surveyed in the preceding chapter is built on the unit of

the province, beginning with the House of Commons. We have reviewed the agreement reached at Confederation that membership in the House of Commons be based on the principle of representation by population. And it is. But this principle is refracted through the prism of the provinces. Indeed, the precise words of the Constitution on the point refer to the "proportionate Representation of the Provinces." So the country is not a single unit out of which electoral districts (or seats) are carved irrespective of provincial boundaries. Instead, electoral districts are assigned on a province-by-province basis.

Theoretically the assignment of districts on a provincial basis is not inconsistent with the principle of representation by population. At the outset, for example, Quebec was made the anchor of the system, and assigned sixty-five seats. That number was divided into the province's population to get an average population per seat, or electoral quotient. The share of seats assigned to the other provinces was determined simply by dividing their respective populations by the electoral quotient. The result was arguably the same as if the country were one electoral unit.

Psychologically speaking, however, the assignment of seats on a province-by-province basis was bound to make provinces think that they "owned" seats and feel protective about them – especially the small provinces. As the decades wore on, and the rate of increase of the populations of Ontario and Quebec outstripped the rate of increase of the populations in the Maritime provinces, concern there mounted. The Maritime provinces faced the loss of seats, both in absolute terms and in relation to the central provinces. Naturally they objected to this fate, since it symbolized the decline of their influence in Ottawa. They gained some ground in 1915 when the Constitution was amended to include the senatorial floor rule, under which no province can have fewer MPs than senators. This is by no means the only rule that has been concocted from time to time to protect provinces from losing seats in the House of Commons. Nevertheless, it is the most important because the senatorial floor is entrenched in the Constitution under the unanimity rule – so that change requires the unanimous consent of the federal and provincial governments – rather than in a statute that Parliament alone can alter.

Understandably, the introduction of such exceptions as the senatorial floor rule has had the effect of moving the distribution of seats further away from the principle of representation by population than otherwise would be the case. The distribution today illustrates the point. At the time of writing there were 301 seats in the House of Commons, distributed as shown in Table 1. In only three of the provinces, Ontario, British Columbia, and Alberta, is the assignment of seats driven solely by population. The rest are protected by special rules.

As required under the Constitution, the assignment of seats must be reviewed and adjusted if necessary in the wake of the decennial census. Following the census in 2001, the assignment of seats was revised such that Ontario, BC, and Alberta will receive additional seats, bringing the new total to 308 seats. This adjustment brings these provinces closer to the principle of representation by population. The situation for the rest of the provinces remains as before,

Table 1

House of Commons seats, 2003

Province/Territory	Seats	Population
Ontario	106	11,410,046
Quebec	75	7,237,479
Nova Scotia	11	908,007
New Brunswick	10	729,498
Manitoba	14	1,119,583
British Columbia	36	3,907,738
Prince Edward Island	4	135,294
Saskatchewan	14	978,933
Alberta	28	2,974,807
Newfoundland and Labrador	7	512,930
Yukon	1	28,674
Northwest Territories	1	37,360
Nunavut	1	26,745
Total	308	30,007,094

Note: Provinces and territories are listed by order of entry into Confederation.
Sources: Elections Canada 2002, 20; 2001 Canadian Census.

however, except that some of them are even more protected. New-foundland and Labrador is the spectacular example. The province's pop-ulation of 568,474 under the 1991 census declined to 512,930 under the 2001 census, by a shocking 10 percent, but it will retain the seven seats it has now (Elections Canada 2002, 20).

What does this say about inclusion and participation? Primarily it says that the provinces and the territories are the key units repre-sented in the House of Commons. No other territorial unit is formally represented there, and no nonterritorial unit is either. It is fair to point out that MPs are not delegates of the provinces and do not act like they are; they are elected as members of the federal political par-ties and they act like partisans. This argument has merit, but two responses are in order. One is that MPs do pay close attention to local and provincial concerns. For example, east coast members are ever alert to the state of the Atlantic fisheries but pay little or no attention to the automotive industry in Quebec and southern Ontario. Conversely, members from Quebec and southern Ontario in whose constituencies the automotive industry is located have no interest in the Atlantic fishery. A second rejoinder is that the political parties necessarily respond to the way in which seats in the House are dis-tributed. They calculate their electoral strategies within a province-based context, paying particular attention to the provinces with the most seats.

The distribution of seats in the House also speaks to the demo-graphic realities of the country. As Table 1 demonstrates, the distri-bution departs from the strict application of the principle of repre-sentation by population. The small provinces are overrepresented in relation to their populations. If population alone were considered, for example, PEI would be entitled to one seat, not four. Still the over-whelming number of seats is concentrated in Ontario and Quebec. This concentration reflects the uneven spread of the population com-bined with the small number of provinces. These simple facts yield a clear picture of the geographic centre of political power in the coun-try – Ontario and Quebec.

The unique trait of federalism to configure political power from geographic units is replicated throughout the institutions of the national government. The twist of regionalism that is used as the basis of representation in the Senate, for example, is a province-based formula by another name. There is equal regional representation, to be sure, but Ontario and Quebec are regions in their own right; the four westernmost provinces are a region, each assigned the same number of senators; and the three Maritime provinces are a region, again each assigned a specific number of senators. For the rest, Newfoundland and Labrador and the territories are assigned their respective complements. Even if the appointed senators arguably incline to a national perspective on issues rather than a provincial one, they are selected on a provincial basis rather than on some other basis.

In the Canadian parliamentary system, the members of the House of Commons comprise the pool out of which the prime minister constructs the cabinet. Therefore the province-based system of representation in the House affects the composition of the cabinet – just as the critics predicted it would, as we saw in the last chapter. According to a conventional rule each of the provinces gets representation in the cabinet, and this is where the importance of PEI's four seats becomes apparent. Those four seats have generated the expectation that the Island will get a cabinet minister, assuming at least one of the MPs is of the right partisan persuasion (Courtney 2001, 30). Such an expectation would be out of the question had the Island only one seat. Of course when no candidate from the prime minister's party has been elected in a given province, the conventional rule is impossible to follow. Even in such cases as these, however, the effort is made to find a representative, often by picking a senator from the province in question. For example, in the general election in 1997 Nova Scotia did not elect any Liberal MPs – nothing like this had happened in the province before. Since the Liberal Party won a majority of the seats in the country, the prime minister named a Liberal senator from the province to represent it in the cabinet.

Of course prime ministers follow other representational requirements when selecting the members of the cabinet, among them religion and gender. The point being made here is that provincial representation matters a lot. One strong indicator is the concept of the
political minister (Bakvis 1991, 7-8). The media routinely refer to the
political minister for the province, meaning the minister through
whom government appointments of individuals from the province
are vetted and through whom federal monies for various local projects are channelled. Generally speaking the political minister from
the province is the senior minister. A very high-profile example
occurred in January 2002 when Prime Minister Chrétien undertook a
major cabinet shuffle and appointed John Manley, previously the
minister of foreign affairs, to the position of deputy prime minister
with responsibility, among other things, for the administration of a
$2 billion infrastructure fund. It was noted with keen interest that
Manley was the new political minister of Ontario.

The Supreme Court of Canada is also affected by the imperative of
provincial representation. Currently there are nine judges on the
court, three of whom by law must come from Quebec. In addition to
the Quebec requirement, the practice has developed according to
which there are three judges from Ontario, two from the Western
provinces and one from the Atlantic provinces (Hogg 1996, 217-18).
This bears an eerie resemblance to the use of provincial and regional
representation in the Senate. It must be stressed that the judges are
not understood to "represent" a province or a region. On the contrary,
in accordance with the principle of judicial independence they are
expected to decide the cases before them strictly on the merits.
Nevertheless the factor of provincial and regional representation is
part of the institutional mix.

The importance of the provinces in the amending formulas cannot
be gainsaid. As indicated in the previous chapter, under the
Constitution the provincial legislatures and Parliament are the only
formal players designated in any of the processes, but this does not
mean they are the only players. Far from it. The last two efforts at
constitutional reform centred on the proposed Meech Lake Accord of

1987, which failed to gain the approval of all of the provincial legislatures and was dropped; and the proposed Charlottetown Accord of 1992, which the first ministers decided to put to a referendum before placing it before the legislatures (assuming it was voted up). The Charlottetown referendum gave the ordinary Canadian voter a crack at the wicket – and a majority voted it down. It is not easy to say whether the referendum is now a required part of the process, albeit an unstated one. What remains certain is that under the Constitution the designated actors in the amending process are Parliament and the provincial legislatures – and no one else.

Finally, by definition the extraconstitutional institutions of executive federalism are built around the provinces, and to a lesser extent the territories. These institutions are not restricted to the elected political leaders, like the prime minister, the premiers, and the territorial leaders (first ministers' conferences) or the premiers and territorial leaders (the Annual Premiers' Conference). In addition the officials in the governments have ongoing meetings. For example, the federal officials of Health Canada meet regularly with their counterparts in the provincial and territorial ministries of health, and the same is replicated throughout the bureaucracy. These meetings are organized on an intergovernmental basis, which means federal-provincial meetings or federal-provincial-territorial meetings. Moreover, and even more interesting, the provinces attend such meetings as formal equals, despite the real inequalities among the provinces in terms of size, wealth, and population.

Who's In: Quebec and National Governing Institutions

Any discussion of the provincial basis of the national governing institutions must include the position of Quebec. In many respects under the Constitution Quebec is the same as the other provinces. For example, the basic juridical equality of the provinces means that each has the same powers to make laws as the others (Milne 1991,

293). Quebec, however, is often said to be a province "pas comme les autres" – unlike the others.

The argument that Quebec is unique rests on two main considerations: some constitutional particulars that distinguish it from the rest of the provinces; and its cultural uniqueness. Of course the constitutional particulars flow from the uniqueness. Among them are the requirement that the province maintain a bilingual regime in its legislature and courts; the requirement that some federally appointed judges be selected from the province; the possession of a civil-law system that is not found in any other province; and different qualifications for senators – Quebec's twenty-four senators are each appointed from one of twenty-four electoral districts of the province. The cultural uniqueness is rooted in the fact that the province is the home of the largest French-speaking community in North America, which comprises some 80 percent of the population.

The question arises whether any of this bears on inclusiveness. Some would say that it does. They would argue that Quebec's uniqueness has given rise to a special status within the federation, "special status" being a code phrase for the perception that the province makes more demands on the system than the other provinces and gets more than its share of the good things available. Then there is the issue of secession. Understandably the French-speaking community in Quebec possesses a strong sense of political cohesiveness that predates the establishment of the country in 1867. More recently this has given rise to a successful political party – the Parti Québécois – that is dedicated to the project of the independence of Quebec. Again some hold that the threat of independence, which might precipitate the breakup of Canada, enables the province to wrest more from the system than would otherwise be possible.

From the standpoint of inclusiveness two points should be made about Quebec. First, the fact of the matter is that under the Constitution the province is not treated in a way that privileges it in terms of inclusion. For example, it is not treated differently from the other provinces in the assignment of seats in the House of Commons. Its assignment is tied to population as much as – if not more than –

the assignment of other provinces. In the Senate, Quebec is in the same category as Ontario, being treated as a region for the purposes of representation. Any perceived "heft" that the province's elected politicians display at the national level is a function of politics rather than the design of the institutions. An example is voting behaviour. It has long been observed that a significant chunk of the province's MPs are usually to be found in the caucus of the governing party (Bakvis and MacPherson 1995, 690). As a result, a strong pool is available for appointment to the cabinet. In addition, the province has supplied an impressive number of prime ministers, five out of the fourteen who held the office in the twentieth century. To repeat, this results from the conduct of politics rather than the institutions themselves.

The second point that must be made about inclusiveness, however, is a matter of symbolic politics, although not the less important for that. Legally speaking, Quebec is as much a part of the Constitution as any other province. Symbolically speaking, it is not. The reason is rooted in the events leading to the adoption of the Constitution Act, 1982, which among other things contains the Canadian Charter of Rights and Freedoms and the formula used to amend the Constitution. As noted in Chapter 3, the Quebec government was unhappy with some aspects of the Charter and the amending formula and therefore refused to join the other provincial governments and the federal government in accepting the act. For their part, these governments were prepared to go ahead without Quebec and did. Altogether it was an unpleasant episode in the history of Canadian federalism. Again, as noted in Chapter 3, the purpose of the failed Meech Lake Accord (1987), which included changes to the Constitution crafted in response to the demands of Quebec, was to gain the public approval of the province to the constitutional developments of 1982.

The failure of the accord, widely supported in Quebec but not else-where in the country, was followed by the débâcle of the Charlottetown Accord, a document that was not as popular in Quebec as its predecessor. These constitutional failures, which many in the province interpreted as a rejection of Quebec by the rest of Canada, set the scene for the provincial election in 1994 of a rejuvenated Parti Québécois, which once again embarked on a drive toward secession. In October 1995 the PQ government held a referendum on the idea of Quebec's independence in the event that Canada turned down a proposal of sovereignty-association between Canada and Quebec. The referendum was a heart-stopper: 49.4 percent voted yes and 50.58 percent voted no. The turnout was an exceedingly high 93.52 percent of the Quebec electorate.

The referendum was a draining affair for Canadians, who could be forgiven for thinking that their country was a hair's breadth from breaking apart and for holding the federal government responsible. For its part, the federal government was shaken by the close vote and determined to get control of matters. A debate ensued about appropriate strategies, some arguing for an aggressive, tough line of refusing to consider the idea of Quebec seceding from Canada, even if the secessionists were to win a referendum; others urged the need to consider alternative ways in which Canada and Quebec might coexist. In the end the government weighed in at the tough end, not by ignoring Quebec but instead by asking the Supreme Court of Canada to rule on the legality of Quebec, or any other province for that matter, choosing to secede unilaterally from Canada following a successful referendum.

In August 1998 the Court handed down its ruling that in the event of a referendum that produced a "clear [yes] answer" to a "clear question" on the desirability of Quebec being independent, the federal and provincial governments would have an obligation to enter into negotiations on the issue with the Quebec government. The Court also admonished both sides to deal with one another in good faith should such negotiations be required. The Court's decision was by no means the end of matters. On the contrary, the Quebec government spun the decision in its favour by stressing the duty to negotiate and the ruling Parti Québécois went on to win the next election. The federal government proved to be no slouch either. It picked up on the Court's notion of a clear answer to a clear question and used it as the rationale for its next move, the Clarity Act, 1999, which effectively empowers the

House of Commons to decide for itself whether a referendum question on independence is clearly worded and whether the answer of the voters is unambiguously in favour of it. In other words, the House is to decide whether the conditions for negotiations have been met. If it decides that they have not been met, then there will be no negotiations.

The Quebec government did not take the Clarity Act lying down. It responded with Bill 99, An Act Respecting the Exercise of the Fundamental Rights and Prerogatives of the Quebec People and the Quebec State, which was adopted by the National Assembly in December 2000. The act stipulates the right of Quebec to design its own referendum question, to run the referendum, and to decide that a simple majority vote determines the result. And for now, this is where things stand in what has become a legal duel between Quebec and Ottawa. As far as Quebec is concerned, the Constitution is unfinished business. Some Quebec federalists who want the province to stay within Canada seek an accommodation with the rest of the country in which the special character or uniqueness of the people of the province is recognized in the Constitution. Others regard such recognition as passé, and are more interested in expanding the province's legislative responsibilities than in finding symbolic phrases to describe its uniqueness. From the standpoint of inclusiveness, a way has not yet been found to wrap the Constitution around Quebec.

Who's In: The Territories and National Governing Institutions

The territories occupy a unique place in the governing institutions of the country. On the one hand, they are not provinces and do not possess the legal rights and privileges accorded to the provinces under the Constitution, chief among which is the exclusive power to legislate on a broad range of subject areas. Instead, they exercise legislative powers that are delegated to them by the federal Parliament. On the other hand, the territorial governments operate within clearly defined boundaries. They have the one overwhelmingly important asset in any federal system: land. This makes them players in the federal system that need to be considered.

At Confederation, provision was made to admit the huge territories of Rupert's Land and the North-Western Territory (essentially the northern part of the continent) into Canada whenever Parliament requested the British government to make the transaction, which it did in 1870. On admission these territories were made subject to the authority of Parliament. Parts of them were used to create Manitoba (1870), the Yukon Territory (1898), and Alberta and Saskatchewan (1905). The remainder was referred to as the Northwest Territories. In 1993 the third territory, Nunavut, was carved out of the Northwest Territories.

In the cases of the Yukon and the Northwest Territories, Parliament has established a governmental structure that consists of a federally appointed commissioner who is responsible to the federal government for the administration of the territory, and an elected council with a term of four years. The commissioner in council – in other words, the commissioner acting on the agreement of the council – is authorized to make laws in relation to a specified number of subjects ranging from the establishment and maintenance of jails to the preservation of game to schools to agriculture. However, the federal government can disallow any law within a year of its passage.

Under the Nunavut Act, 1993, a somewhat different form of government was established for the newest territory. Again the commissioner is appointed by the federal government and reports to it. Nunavut's elected Legislative Assembly does not have a fixed term of four years but instead, like Parliament and the provincial legislative assemblies, is assigned a maximum term of five years, before which time new elections to the assembly must be held. In addition, there is an executive council, or cabinet, which consists of members appointed by the commissioner on the recommendation of the Legislative Assembly. Finally, the subject areas assigned to the Legislative Assembly go beyond those assigned to the other territorial governments. Thus the assembly can legislate to preserve the use of the Inuktitut language. It can also authorize the commissioner and other officials to enter into intergovernmental agreements.

The mention of intergovernmental agreements raises the point made in the last chapter about the inclusion of the territorial governments in meetings with the provincial and federal governments. This development is important because these meetings, which are the stuff of intergovernmental relations, are a prominent feature of Canadian federalism. Although the territorial governments are not on the same level as the others from the constitutional standpoint, still they are players who can make their views known in these vital decision-making circles. And they are vital, especially in recent years when the effort has been made to pursue a collaborative form of federalism that appears to be more appropriate than intergovernmental conflict in an era when governments need to work together in order to accomplish their policy goals. Prominent examples of agreements that have been reached include the Agreement on Internal Trade (AIT) in 1995, signed by the federal, provincial, and territorial governments (then only the Yukon and Northwest Territories); the National Child Benefit (NCB) agreement in 1998, signed by the federal, provincial, and territorial governments but not Quebec, although Quebec participates in its implementation; and the Social Union Framework Agreement (SUFA) in 1999, signed by the federal government, nine provincial premiers (the Quebec premier declined to sign), and the three territorial governments. Whatever the merits of such agreements, their scope and significance demonstrate how important it is for the territorial governments to participate in the negotiations.

One of the most striking aspects of the territorial governments is their relationship to Aboriginal communities. The demographic figures collected in the 1996 census show that in the Yukon (population of 30,000) the ratio is 20 percent Aboriginal to 80 percent non-Aboriginal; in the Northwest Territories (population of 41,000) it is 48 percent to 52 percent; and in Nunavut (population of 28,000) the Inuit constitute 84 percent of the population. Thus in Nunavut the territorial government, although a public government, is in practice an example of Inuit self-government.

In addition to the demographic facts, which imply a strong role for Aboriginal peoples in the governments of the territories, there is the question of land. The Canadian government has negotiated a number of land claim agreements covering land in the territories with First Nations and Aboriginal groups. These agreements vary, but typically they involve the transfer of legislative powers from the federal government to the Aboriginal community concerned. The negotiation process is far from complete, but it is further along in the North than in, say, Nova Scotia, and it covers vast areas. In conceptualizing the territorial governments, then, it is essential to think about the concluded and pending land claim agreements, since these agreements spell out forms of Aboriginal government. Of course this is also true for the federal and provincial governments, which suggests that it is past time to turn to the issue of Aboriginal governance.

Who Is on the Way In?

It would be easy to classify Aboriginal peoples under the "who's out" category on the basis of their experience of oppression, marginalization, and poverty in British North America and then in Canada. Certainly issues of oppression, marginalization, and poverty remain to be addressed. Nevertheless in recent years the entrenchment of Aboriginal and treaty rights in the Constitution, the Aboriginal drive toward self-government, and the Aboriginal pursuit of land claim agreements as well as treaty renovation together have produced a situation that bids fair to transform Canadian federalism from a system of divided government (federal and provincial) into a system of multi-layered governance. Now is a time of transition: Aboriginal governments are reorganizing and changing, many land claim agreements are under negotiation, and the relationship between Aboriginal governments, groups, and individuals, on the one hand, and the other governments in the country, on the other, is still developing.

Before turning to the issue of inclusion in the federal system, it is helpful to supply some context, beginning with the size of the Aboriginal population, which the 1996 census placed at about 2.8 percent of the population of the country. In each of the Atlantic provinces, Quebec, and Ontario the percentage is lower than that. In Manitoba and Saskatchewan it is 11.7 and 11.4 percent respectively; in British Columbia and Alberta it is 3.8 and 4.6 percent respectively; and in the territories, as noted above, the percentages are more substantial still. Finally the growth rate of the Aboriginal population is said to be two to three times higher than that of the population as a whole (Cairns 2000, 27-9; Greater Vancouver Regional District 2003).

As noted earlier, at Confederation the inclusion of the Aboriginal population in the federal system amounted to the fact that "Indians, and Lands reserved for the Indians" were among the responsibilities assigned to the federal Parliament. This provision remains in the Constitution. Under it Parliament legislated an administrative regime that for well over a century reached an Aboriginal population defined as status Indians resident on reserves. Non-status, landless Aboriginal people were left out of this system and remained instead simply part of the larger society. The report of the Royal Commission on Aboriginal Peoples (1996) is an authoritative indictment of the ills of the federal regime as well as the situation of those outside of it. The report also emphasizes, however, that throughout the long dark night, Aboriginal peoples maintained that they never surrendered their sovereignty and insisted that their historic and ongoing relationship with the British Crown, sometimes encapsulated in treaties and sometimes not, is a nation-to-nation relationship. The notion of sovereignty past, present, and future is their political anchor, and a particularly weighty one when combined with land.

In 1982 existing Aboriginal and treaty rights were entrenched in the Constitution, treaty rights being defined to include rights already gained through land claim agreements and rights to be acquired in future agreements. In addition the term "Aboriginal" was specified to include the Indian, Métis, and Inuit populations. These important constitutional developments, combined with a more receptive view of

Aboriginal claims taken by the Canadian courts, set the stage for such progress in the adjustment of the relationship between Aboriginals and non-Aboriginals as has been made to date. This progress is uneven and varied, and the end is by no means in sight. As a result, it is not easy to get a grip on the situation from the standpoint of inclusion in the federal system. A key distinction to keep in mind, however, is between land-based Aboriginal communities, whose land effectively gains them purchase in the federal system, and non-status Indians and Métis, who have no equivalent land base, although in northern Alberta the Métis exercise some powers of local government over eight settlements (Cairns 2002, 27). In *R. v. Powley* (2003), the Métis recently gained judicial recognition of important hunting and fishing rights in and around Sault Ste. Marie.

In Canadian law, the right to self-government of Aboriginal peoples is inherent and continues to exist unless it was expressly given up by them. It is one thing to assert a right in speech, however, and another to act on it. Aboriginal self-government is much harder to visualize off a land base than on it. In practice title to land is a condition of self-government, and self-government spells automatic inclusion in the federal system. Politically speaking this is why land claims are so important to Aboriginal peoples. Some Aboriginal communities signed treaties with the British Crown long ago that reserved lands to them. Many did not. In 1997 in *Delgamuukw* v. *British Columbia* the Supreme Court of Canada ruled that Aboriginals who have not signed treaties can press a land claim by demonstrating that their ancestors occupied the land in question before the Europeans arrived.

Anyone who expected a rush of settlements in the wake of *Delgamuukw* was proven to be naïve. A lot is at stake – cash, control of natural resources, and therefore political power – and the process is contentious and slow. When negotiations stall, the Aboriginal parties resort to the legal system. Thus in March 2002 the Haida finally went to court to press their claim to their ancestral lands in the Queen Charlotte Islands (Haida Gwaii) northwest of Vancouver Island, and to the waters surrounding them, which happen to contain huge oil and gas reserves. This is an example of a comprehensive claim based on unextinguished Aboriginal title, or title to the land that was never ceded to anyone or any government. Incidentally many other BC Aboriginal communities never signed treaties either and have yet to negotiate land claim agreements successfully with the federal government. Taken together, these claims cover much of the province.

Still, there is one example in British Columbia of a recently negotiated treaty: the Nisga'a Treaty. The Nisga'a successfully negotiated a self-government agreement with the federal and BC governments that covers an impressive bit of real estate along the coast of the province. The particulars of the treaty are not important here so much as the point that the Nisga'a alone have specified rights and powers in relation to a part of the province. Arguably this makes the Nisga'a a third order of government. The Nisga'a example is somewhat different from the Inuit of Nunavut, who settled on the option of a territorial government. Should they lose control of the government as a result of an influx of non-Inuit residents, then they could resort to the route taken by the Nisga'a and negotiate a self-government agreement in their traditional lands. Yet another variation on the theme concerns the northern Innu in Quebec, who have negotiated a treaty proposal with the Quebec government that assigns them specified governing rights over a defined area in the north of the province and a slice of the economic rents flowing from any resource development in the area.

Another land claim and self-government agreement was initialled in August 2003 between the federal government and the Dogrib, one of the five tribes of the Dene people of northern Canada. The land at issue covers about 39,000 square kilometres in the Northwest Territories. Under the agreement, the Dogrib are assigned ownership of the resources of the area, a significant degree of control over the development of these resources, and entitlement to revenue streams from these resources. The Tli Cho government, as it is called, is made up of elected councillors, half of whom must be Dogrib, and a chief, who also must be Dogrib. The Tli Cho government is focused on the development and regulation of area's natural resources, and replaces previous Aboriginal councils and municipal councils. For its part, the government of the Northwest Territories retains the authority to administer such services as health and education in the area. In addition to the agreement with the Dogrib are concluded agreements with other communities and agreements still in the process of negotiation.

As well as comprehensive land claims, specific claims or grievances about the federal government's administration of particular treaties remain to be sorted out. So there is much ongoing and much to be accomplished. The only sure point is this: the federal system has to accommodate a third order of government that is land-based, and it can do so precisely because it is already a system of land-based governments in the provinces and the territories. This is self-rule – the very foundation of the system.

Who's Out: Aboriginal Individuals off the Land

In another category altogether, it seems, are non-status Indians and Aboriginal individuals who are not members of a community with land or a claim to land. These individuals are not included in the federal system as Aboriginal individuals. Instead they are included as individuals, no different from any non-Aboriginal who resides in a province or territory. The federal government has an urban Aboriginal strategy for cities with significant numbers of Aboriginals. Under the strategy, the government finances various projects designed to respond to the problems that urban Aboriginals face (Federal Interlocutor for Métis and Non-Status Indians 2003). Their plight, however, is sufficiently difficult that, at least in Winnipeg, some thought is being given to carving out space for them within the city in the form of an "urban reserve" (Desnomie 2003). This option is an attempt to solve the problem of the lack of a land base by establishing one.

Aboriginal individuals without a land base can be considered to be included in the federal system only if all Aboriginal peoples are represented formally in the institutions of the central government, especially Parliament. But they are not. Anyone with aspirations to get to

Parliament needs to compete with non-Aboriginals to do so, and it is a tough haul. Since Confederation hardly more than a dozen Aboriginals have been elected to the House of Commons, and fewer than that number have been appointed to the Senate (Courtney 2001, 217).

Recently there has been recognition that the inclusion of Aboriginal peoples in elected institutions at the federal level requires making space under the rules that govern representation there. The Royal Commission on Electoral Reform and Party Financing (the Lortie Commission) in 1991 recommended the establishment of electoral districts in the House of Commons to be set aside for Aboriginal voters only. Such districts could obviously be geographically based in areas populated by Aboriginal communities. Or they could be provincewide, in which case Aboriginals residing anywhere in the province could register to vote in them. Later that same year a different idea surfaced in the Charlottetown Accord for guaranteed Aboriginal representation in the Senate, seats in the House to be negotiated at a later date. Since Aboriginal leaders were closely involved in the negotiations of the failed accord, this idea deserves attention. In 1996 the Royal Commission on Aboriginal Peoples proposed something different again, namely a third chamber of Parliament elected by Aboriginal peoples and charged with advising the House and the Senate on matters affecting them. Clearly, then, there are ways of including the Aboriginal peoples in the federal government. Certainly they are barely there now.

Who's Out: Cities

As mentioned at the outset of the chapter, city governments have no independent constitutional footing. Instead they come under the category of municipal institutions and are the responsibility of the provinces. Therefore in terms of the Constitution, the great metropolitan centres of Toronto, Vancouver, and Montreal are the equals of the charming Atlantic town of Yarmouth, Nova Scotia. And they are all constitutionally inferior to Prince Edward Island. As a result, and following the analysis used thus far, the inescapable conclusion is that the cities – as cities – are not independent players in the federal system. What does this mean for inclusion?

First, the constitutional status of the cities as a subject of legislation of the provinces means that there are no direct institutional links between the federal government and the cities. The federal cabinet contains no Department of Cities. The government of Prime Minister Pierre Elliott Trudeau once established a Department of Urban Affairs, but it was a short-lived experiment much reviled by some of the provinces. The federal government can spend money on cities, however; it can spend money on almost anything it likes. Thus far the spending has been episodic. For example, when Halifax hosted the G7 Summit in 1998, the federal government transferred funds to the city to help it with the expenditures entailed by such an event. But this was a one-time transaction, not spending tied to a long-term program.

The cash-strapped cities are currently looking for dependable revenue streams, and the federal government has deeper pockets than the provinces. The federal government toyed with the idea of assigning to the cities an unspecified portion of the federal fuel tax. This would have been a significant decision because it would be nearly impossible to reverse and would fly in the face of the provinces, the standard position of which is that any federal spending on cities should flow through them. The government abandoned the idea and instead has offered the cities a full rebate of the sales tax (GST) on goods and services purchased by them. The offer is estimated to amount to $7 billion over the next decade (Bueckert 2004). Still, no spending would affect the legal position of the cities as the creatures of the provinces.

A second point to keep in mind is that no electoral districts in the House of Commons are set aside for cities. Of course some MPs represent districts within cities, and districts that run across city boundaries and into adjacent suburbs or rural areas. But none represents a city, simply. MPs who represent districts within cities are regarded as being urban members rather than being rural members, but that degree of categorization is as far as it goes. There is no representation of the cities in the Senate, either. The obvious conclusion to be drawn, then, is that cities as entities in and of themselves are not formally included in the federal system. And this is despite the fact that they are territorial entities and therefore could be so included. The problem for the cities – or at least for those who think that the cities ought to be included in the system in some fashion – is that the provinces got there first.

Conclusion

The territorial organization of communities for the purpose of government is important for a number of reasons. To begin, it means that communities are not organized in some other way, like religion or ethnicity. Instead people have to think about their communities and the representativeness of their governments in geographic terms. The province is the key organizational component in the makeup of Parliament. This is why issues like the representation of the provinces in the Senate are so important. Moreover, geography implies boundaries, some of which are more enduring than others. Provincial boundaries are enduring. Once settled, they stay that way unless adjacent provinces pursue change, in which case they need to proceed formally to make a change under the terms of the Constitution. The boundaries of the municipalities, including the cities, are not enduring, and herein lies a cautionary democratic tale.

In the 1990s, when governments found themselves fighting seemingly intractable deficits and therefore a growing debt burden, they looked everywhere to save money, including the size of the governing units. The provinces themselves were not about to amalgamate, but the municipalities were a different kettle of fish. A provincial government could order the amalgamation of specified municipalities within its boundaries should it choose to do so. The argument for municipal amalgamation then bruited about was to save money by streamlining the administrative delivery of local services. Accordingly, in Nova Scotia the newly elected government of Premier John Savage made the decision to amalgamate the cities of Halifax, Bedford, and Dartmouth and the semirural municipality of Halifax into an entity called the Halifax Regional Metropolis, or HRM for short. There was a short, sharp little battle over the decision, but in the end the municipal leaders could do nothing except get on with the job of combining four separate local governments into one, large local government.

Some democratic issues involved in this matter deserve attention. One is the fact that the voters never had a look at it. The idea of amalgamation was not on the agenda of the 1993 election that ushered in the Savage government, and the government declined to hold a referendum on it. (So too did the Ontario government in 1997 when it chose to amalgamate the municipal governments of metropolitan Toronto into a single government. The City of Toronto held a vote on the issue to which the province paid no attention.) Another issue is the upset to settled practice that an event like amalgamation entails. In the Nova Scotia case, the four previous municipal governments had been that way for decades, and citizens knew how to deal with them. Knowing how to deal with familiar governments is an asset. When things are turned upside down, citizens need to readjust to the new order, which amounts to a transaction cost that they pay. Finally there is the issue of size. Inevitably one new council is not the same as four old ones. The geographic unit of representation for the purpose of the election of members of the council of the HRM is much larger than any of the units under the old system. So not only do citizens have to learn to deal with a new organization, but there are many more of them per councillor than before.

Canadian federalism, not federalism per se, is the reason for the subordination of the municipalities to the provinces. Nevertheless, there is no getting around the fact that in federal systems inclusion is a matter of geography, and geography implies boundaries. Boundaries fix communities for the purpose of government. Consequently boundaries have a deep impact on the quality of governing practices, and in particular on how democratic they are. Boundaries define who and how many are included for what purposes. As with inclusion, so with participation, which is the subject of the next chapter of the audit.

CHAPTER 4

- Federalism organizes people out of the system as well as organizing them into it.

- Canadian federalism is province based.

- As far as Quebec is concerned, the Constitution is unfinished business.

- The Aboriginal drive toward self-government and pursuit of land claim agreements as well as treaty renovation together may transform Canadian federalism from a system of divided government (federal and provincial) into a system of multilayered governance.

DEMOCRATIC AUDIT OF PARTICIPATION IN THE FEDERAL SYSTEM 5

Inclusion is a necessary condition of participation in the federal system. Anyone who is not "at the table" cannot participate. On the other hand, inclusion is not a sufficient condition of full participation or equal participation with others. There are degrees of participation. Some citizens are at the heart of the action; some operate at its margins. The democratic audit of participation in the federal system undertaken in this chapter is meant to lay bare such realities.

Before proceeding, there are a few issues to sort out, beginning with a reminder of who is meant by "participants." The participants are the governments, on the one hand, and everyone else, on the other hand, including individuals and organizations. Then there is the meaning of the term "participation." This implies more than voting, otherwise consulting the surveys of voter turnout at elections would suffice to determine the state of participation in the political process. As the term is used here, participation refers to engagement in the policy-making processes between elections. Thus the audit assesses the opportunities and the obstacles facing individuals and organizations that choose to participate in the federal system between elections.

It must be stressed that the audit singles out the ways in which the federal system itself affects participation. The audit is focused on the system rather than on the characteristics of the participants. As the audit suggests, the opportunities for participation that the system yields are significant and ought not to be brushed aside. At the same time, it is abundantly clear that the system also raises some obstacles that prospective participants, be they lone individuals or organizations, need to hurdle. The greatest obstacle of all is the arena of participation from which citizens are excluded altogether: the arena of executive federalism that is reserved to the governments themselves. Many describe executive federalism as the lifeblood of the federal system. Like the lifeblood of individuals, it is more or less invisible to the eye – or to the eye of the average citizen. But it is no less important for that. On the contrary, from the standpoint of the participation of citizens in politics, executive federalism is the most important feature of the federal system.

Opportunities for Citizen Participation in the Federal System

As was pointed out in Chapter 1, most people participate in the political system only in elections. Periodically they elect the federal, provincial, territorial, municipal, and Aboriginal governments. Thus they participate in an indirect form of democracy by electing others to govern for them. They exact the accountability of the elected officials by choosing to retain them at the next election or to vote them out of office.

In recent times, particularly in the older democracies, some impatience has been expressed with the notion that democracy is nothing more than the vote. To equate democracy with the vote seems a thin idea that carries the unfortunate implication that citizens are rightly shut out of the political process between elections – in other words during the period in which decision making takes place. The fact that the political parties and the candidates rarely offer detailed policy platforms during election campaigns only reinforces the suspicion that elections, however exciting, are the tip of the proverbial iceberg, and that citizens need to extend their political engagement beyond such events. And they do. They protest in the streets; join political parties in the hope of influencing their policies and their choice of candidates; join interest groups in order to lobby governments for or against particular policies; publicize their views in the media in order to influence public opinion; go to court to enforce rights against governments that are held to have violated them; and so on. What is the significance of the federal system for all of this?

The federal system imposes a particular kind of structure on citizen participation, rather like the impact of the design of a house on the way the occupants live in it. Possibly the most widely noted feature of the system that is thought to encourage participation is related to scale. The federal system has different levels of government, among which are elected local governments. Elected local governments are smaller than the elected national government, and smaller governments are easier for citizens to engage than larger governments – or so common sense would suggest.

Undoubtedly there is much to the commonsense view. As a general rule smaller governments are easier to access than larger governments. There are fewer people with whom to deal; the organization of the government is less complex; and the offices are likely to be located in one spot. In PEI, for instance, the provincial government is much smaller than the governments of some Canadian cities, serving a population of just over 135,000. The capital city of Charlottetown is no further than an hour's drive from the furthest reaches of the province. The provincial legislature has twenty-seven seats, and the average number of electors per district is just over 5,000. The logistics suggest that it cannot be difficult for any Islander to participate at the provincial level, either as a member of the political parties, as an individual, or as a member of an organization seeking to shape the public-policy agenda. And what is true at the provincial level holds many times over for the municipal level: the largest government, Charlottetown, serves a population of some 35,000.

PEI is obviously an extreme example of small size. Nevertheless, even the larger provinces with sizable governmental institutions are blanketed with municipal governments of varying sizes, many of them easily within the participatory reach of the average resident. Of course what is in reach is not necessarily what is sought. A resident of Ontario who is concerned about a social-welfare issue that is the responsibility of the provinces needs to deal with the government at Queen's Park, which is a formidable apparatus by Canadian standards, and not the town council. Scale is no help there. But in addition to scale, there is the factor of time.

Generally speaking, the development of public policies in federal systems is a slow process. It can take decades to generate sufficient agreement to adopt a particular policy. To some extent this depends on the level at which the decision needs to be made. Obviously at the federal level the threshold of agreement is high, since the nation is involved, not merely one province or territory. An outsized example is the amending formula, a topic on which the federal and provincial governments began to confer in 1927. They finally adopted a formula in 1982. But no one would suggest that decisions routinely take fifty-five years to reach. The point is simply that on many national issues the threshold of agreement is high, there are lots of entry points into the process, and as a result the process takes time. These entry points are avenues of citizen participation.

The factor of time may well be most noticeable at the federal level, and less so at the provincial and municipal levels. Moreover, other factors in addition to the federal system affect the length of time that it takes to reach a decision at any level of government, such as the nature and importance of the issue in question. Another aspect of the federal system is unique to it and serves as an encouragement of citizen participation: the demonstration effect.

Provinces, cities, towns, rural municipalities – all of these units can serve as public-policy laboratories that demonstrate the practical advantages and disadvantages of policy options. One current example unfolding at the municipal level is the use of chemical sprays designed to rid residential and commercial lawns and gardens of pests. Public concern is increasing about the toxic side effects of such products for people, animals, and plants. In the summer of 2001 enough Halifax residents agitated for a ban on specified chemical sprays to convince the elected council to impose one, although not after considerable and anxious debate among those for and against the idea. Interested residents in other urban centres in the country have taken note of these developments as well as court decisions upholding the authority of local councils to take such actions, which a growing number of them are doing.

Another current example on the environmental front concerns the disposal of garbage. Halifax is the first city of any size in Canada to require residents to separate waste into recyclables, compostable materials, noncompostable materials, and newspapers. Residents place the compostable refuse into so-called green bins, which are picked up at regular intervals along with the noncompostable and recyclable refuse. Environmental activists and municipal officials in other cities have been studying the Halifax model as they make plans for changes in their own systems of garbage disposal.

An interesting prospect in terms of the demonstration effect that is unfolding at the provincial level concerns the system used through-out the country to elect officials to public office. That system is the first-past-the-post system, or the horse race, in which the candidate with the most votes (not necessarily a majority of the votes) wins. For decades, the few critics of the system were to be found in the groves of academe and no one paid them any attention. Times change, how-ever, and an increasing number of people appear to be less than enthusiastic about the system, preferring instead to see the adoption of a more proportional system of representation. Some are going to court, charging that the system is a breach of the democratic and equality rights guaranteed in the Canadian Charter of Rights and Freedoms. In PEI and British Columbia, others are working to get the legislatures to adopt a proportional system. Indeed, these two provin-cial governments have responded by establishing formal processes to study the issue and consult the public about it. If one of the provinces were to adopt some form of proportional representation, then the rest of the country could watch the experiment. These kinds of opportunities afforded by the federal system are an encouragement of citizen participation in political life. They enable citizens to drive change.

Obstacles to Citizen Participation in the Federal System

The framework of the federal system also imposes costs on citizen participation in political life, beginning with a knowledge cost. At the most basic level, individuals and organizations in pursuit of a policy objective need to decide which level of government to tackle, and this decision depends on the policy. Anyone who wants to get involved in the offshore fishery must deal with the federal government, because it has the responsibility for the offshore fishery. Anyone interested in curriculum issues in public schools needs to deal with the provincial government. Anyone who wants to get a residential street repaired must deal with the municipal government. Often more than one level of government is active in a particular area of public policy, in which case the individual or association pursuing an objective in that area is faced with a very complex governmental situation. An excellent example is the construction of wharves on the seacoast: an individual who decides to build a wharf on his property needs a daunting array of permits to do so, including construction permits from the municipality in which he resides; transport permits from the province in the event that the wharf lies off a public road; environmental permits from the province, which is responsible for the integrity of the shoreline; and permits from the federal government, which is concerned to keep the channel clear for navigation. Naturally the unsuspecting wharf builder needs to figure out all of this for himself, since no handy guide to the process is made available to the public.

Another cost of participation that is imposed by the federal system, particularly for associations, is organizational complexity. National associations often find that they need provincial and territorial branches for various reasons. Aside from the sheer size of the country, the differences among the regions virtually ensure that one policy cannot apply uniformly everywhere and that debate is required before an organization can settle on a position acceptable to the membership. Another reason, however, is the federal system itself, especially when the issue with which an organization deals has multiple dimensions. Environmental and feminist organizations fall into this category, since they pursue issues for which all governments have responsibilities. At Confederation there was no subject matter called "the environment" or "women's issues" that was distributed among the governments, and therefore activists in these areas need to operate at all levels of the system, hardly an easy task.

Finally, and as a consequence of the preceding considerations, there are time and expense costs. It takes time to figure out how the system works, to generate consensus throughout a far-flung organization, and to deal with layers of government, no matter how helpful the officials themselves. And time is money – which is a quick way to summarize the enormous expenses that are built into the effort to engage governments. The expenses that individuals and organizations face are easy to list: travel; communications; any professional services that might be required, like legal or media services; and so on. There might have been a time long ago when the quiet lobbying of an elected official was enough to generate a shift in a particular government policy, but that is not a realistic proposition for citizen participation today.

In the final analysis, then, those who choose to participate in the political system beyond the level of voting in elections need to pay the costs that are imposed by the organizational complexity of the federal system. Such costs can be expected to depress the level of citizen participation. Moreover, even for those who are prepared and able to pay, another arena of political life exists above and beyond the individual governments: the intergovernmental arena, or executive federalism, which is essentially reserved to the governments themselves.

Executive Federalism

Let us recall Smiley's definition (1980, 91) of executive federalism as "the relations between elected and appointed officials of the two levels of government" in federal-provincial interactions and interprovincial interactions. The term "government" is used precisely in this definition to mean the elected representatives in the legislature who are also members of the cabinet, and their officials (the executive), as opposed to the elected representatives who are not members of the cabinet. In contemplation is the range of meetings that are held between such officials, from the prime minister and the premiers; to the federal and provincial ministers in a particular area, like agriculture or health; to federal and provincial public servants in a particular area; to the provincial premiers and their officials. Sometimes these meetings are trilevel, and include officials at the municipal level.

Chapter 3 described some of the better-known examples of the genre, in particular the meetings of the political leaders, like the first ministers' conferences (FMCs), which include the prime minister and the provincial premiers; the less formal first ministers' meetings, in the past few years expanded to include the territorial leaders as well; and the Annual Premiers' Conference, with the territorial leaders also in attendance. They are often described as "summit" meetings because they are attended by those at the top of the political world. There are also regional meetings of the premiers, like the Western Premiers' Conference; or the Conference of New England Governors and Eastern Canadian Premiers, which includes Quebec and the Atlantic provinces on the Canadian side. A notch down are the meetings at the ministerial level. The most august example is surely the meetings of the finance ministers and deputy ministers, eye-glazing events not especially well covered by the media unless a fight is expected on some issue or other.

Speaking of the media, it is understandable that they choose to cover only the summit meetings, which are less about humdrum business than about very significant business, or no business but much political posturing. Examples of significant business abound. As has already been mentioned, the first formal FMC (then called the Dominion-Provincial Conference) was held in 1906 to discuss the financial relations between the two levels of government, the provinces predictably demanding more than the federal government was prepared to give. Thus was struck a theme that has endured. At the next conference, not held until 1918, the governments dealt with the issues of reconstruction that loomed at the close of the First World War. When the Second World War ended, a series of conferences were held at which the governments reached the agreements necessary to launch the construction of the welfare state. The practice continues to yield results, as indicated by the agreements noted in the previous chapter.

Equally significant have been the FMCs on constitutional issues, often the occasion of high drama as well as academic debate. These meetings were staples of the political scene in the 1960s and 1970s. Even when the principals failed to reach agreement on anything, as commonly occurred, the meetings served to prime the ongoing public debate that is often needed before sufficient public consensus for change can emerge. As discussed previously, agreement (Quebec excepted) was eventually reached in 1981 on major changes, including the adoption of an amending formula and an entrenched bill of rights, both of which are contained in the Constitution Act, 1982. The sequels, first on the Meech Lake Accord and then the Charlottetown Accord, were dramatic failures fit for the closest media attention, which they received.

However fascinating the political dramas might be, they ought not to obscure the meat-and-potatoes side of executive federalism that is often required to enable the first ministers to accomplish something. This is the complex process of intergovernmental negotiations among officials that precede the summit meetings, like the lengthy negotiations preparatory to the 1999 signing of the Social Union Framework Agreement (SUFA) that took place between the relevant federal and provincial departments of government. The history of that document is an interesting example of how summit politics can play out in unexpected ways. In the mid-1990s, the federal government instituted spending cuts in earnest in order to get the recurring annual deficits under control. Finding themselves with less to spend on social programs, the premiers sought to develop a common front to challenge the way in which the federal government's financial policies were driving social policy. They were looking for long-term and reliable federal spending commitments that would enable them to plan ahead with confidence that the money would be there. Otherwise, they said, they would be obliged to retrench on programs, like health care, that are very popular with Canadians. There was a good deal of political noise, and the premiers managed to get Ottawa to negotiate the issue. The eventual result was the SUFA, essentially a statement of the principles that are understood to govern the delivery of social programs as well as a blueprint of the cooperative process to be undertaken to amend them or initiate a new program.

A skeptic might point out that the statement of principles was a statement of the status quo, which is why the Quebec premier declined to sign it. In other words, the provinces had gained nothing in the end. Possibly worse than that, since the federal government managed to defuse provincial discontent within the confines of a remarkably dull document. However, one of the achieved objectives of the SUFA was the establishment of a dispute-settlement mechanism in health care — which shows just how contentious that issue is. Under the Constitution the provinces are responsible for the delivery of health care, but they rely on federal revenue transfers to pay part of the cost. For its part, the federal government has attached conditions to transfers in the form of standards of health care administration that are articulated in the Canada Health Act. Health care for Canadians is required to be publicly administered and funded, comprehensive, portable, and universal. Further, the provinces are prohibited from imposing user fees for health services or permitting health care providers to bill patients directly (extra billing). Meanwhile the costs of health care spiral annually, and so provinces seeking innovative ways to address the problem have come up against — and tried to get around — the constraints of the federal standards.

Such is the background of the dispute-settlement mechanism. The issue is so charged, however, that the mechanism remained a concept until April 2002, when the provinces (except Quebec) finally agreed to the establishment of a three-person panel to settle disputes between them and the federal government about the Canada Health Act. The premier of Alberta, the "point man" for the provinces on the issue, accepted Ottawa's proposal on their behalf (Canadian Press 2002).

Whether the dispute-settlement mechanism ultimately amounts to anything is an open question, health care being such a contentious area for the governments. In the meantime, the idea of a national health council is being championed by the federal government and reviled by several of the provinces, especially Alberta. At a first ministers' meeting held in February 2003, Prime Minister Chrétien won the provinces' approval of a joint health council that would monitor the health care system and report to taxpayers on its status. Not until September of the same year did the governments finally agree to the establishment of the council that will undertake the work. Again, whether it will amount to much is an open question.

Contemplating such examples, it seems that executive federalism has echoes of international relations. The premiers often use their annual conferences to try to develop common positions with which to confront the federal government. Canadians often read about their federal and provincial governments sitting around a table, seeming to negotiate as equals, rather as if they were sovereign nations. Sometimes they see this on television. The spectacle is a peculiarity of Canadian federalism, for reasons that are worth briefly exploring, the first and most obvious being the strength and vigour of the provincial governments.

The provinces are much stronger players in the system than those who framed the Constitution ever anticipated. There are only ten provinces, after all, so none is about to get lost in the shuffle. And one is Quebec, the cultural uniqueness of which ensures that its government will steadfastly protect the exclusive powers and privileges of the provinces under the Constitution, even if any of the others should falter on that score. Moreover, the provinces are responsible for the administration of programs that are extremely important to Canadians, like health care and education. The fact that they always claim not to have enough money to do the job, and demand more from the federal government, is neither here nor there. Or perhaps it is relevant, since the need of the provinces for more tax dollars drives them to negotiate with the federal government, which has ampler access to tax revenues than they do. In other words, this dynamic drives executive federalism, particularly when combined with the understandable interest of the federal government in the administration of policies that Canadians value.

Another reason for the development of executive federalism is the country's parliamentary system of government. Canada was the first country in the world to combine parliamentary government and federalism. The point has already been made that the framers of the Constitution, thinking in parliamentary rather than federal terms, did their best to model the Parliament of Canada after the British Parliament. In the design of the Senate, they were mindful of the House of Lords rather than the American Senate. As a result, the Senate has not functioned as a chamber that is representative of the provinces but instead as a chamber of sober second thought about legislative proposals sent to it from the House of Commons. The cabinet has picked up the representative function to some extent, as discussed in Chapter 3 – but informally and uncertainly, since the make-up of any cabinet is unpredictable. The bottom line is that no body within the federal government is designed to represent the provinces or to speak for them in federal councils, which leaves the provincial governments as the singular agents of provincial concerns, not just in the provincial capitals but at the federal level as well. This situation also drives the need for an arena like executive federalism in which the provincial governments speak directly to the federal government.

A third aspect of the parliamentary system feeds executive federalism, and it has to do with the dominance of the executive in the system. Certainly in Canada as in parliamentary systems elsewhere, the engine of the system is the political executive, meaning the prime minister (or premier) and the cabinet, who together almost always dominate the legislature. The reason is the disciplined character of Canadian political parties. The governing party (which commands the majority of members in the legislature) can always count on the loyalty of its members. This feature of the system makes it easy and natural for the federal and provincial executives to meet and negotiate with one another, unencumbered by legislatures that exact much in the way of accountability from them.

The reasons just advanced to explain the development of executive federalism are institutional reasons. The design of the federal and parliamentary institutions has clearly encouraged officials to deal with one another in intergovernmental meetings rather than in some other way. Before leaving the issue, however, it is tempting to speculate on the impact of something less concrete than an institution, namely, the political culture. Since the establishment of the country at Confederation, the political elites have determined the country's constitutional arrangements and momentous public policies without recourse to the voters unless they had a strategic reason to consult them. An excellent example is Prime Minister Mackenzie King's choice to put the issue of military conscription in the Second World War to the voters in a referendum. The outcome was not in doubt, but he wanted to be absolved by the Quebec voters who opposed the idea from the responsibility of ordering conscription when the time came to do so; he could say that his hand had been forced. In the nation's history, the norm has been no public consultation outside of elections, which are rarely fought on specific policy issues anyway. Very recently there have been glimmers of change, the leading example being the referendum on the Charlottetown Accord. Nonetheless, such an initiative is still the exception rather than the rule. The rule is the dominance of governmental elites in decision making, and public deference to the results. Executive federalism is a fitting practice in such a cultural context.

This reference to the political culture gives the game away as far as the audit is concerned. It is no surprise to find that on any objective analysis, the arena of executive federalism is a damper on democratic participation. All that remains is to show why.

The Impact of Executive Federalism on Democratic Participation

To employ the blunt terminology of the sporting world – it's a shut-out. Nothing has changed since Smiley (1979, 108) wrote that executive federalism "contributes to an unduly low level of citizen participation in public affairs." The reason is not the "federalism" part of the phrase so much as the "executive" part. As has already been indicated, much of the business of the federation is carried out in the ongoing meetings of the governments – meetings between the first ministers, ministers, and civil servants. These meetings mostly are held behind closed doors. They are scheduled when necessary rather than at predictable intervals. They are exclusive, by invitation only. And no mechanism of accountability is built into the process. If something is produced at the end of the negotiation, it has the status of a fait accompli. How would the ordinary person participate in any of this?

There are only two avenues of citizen participation, direct or indirect. Direct participation is out of the question. It is simply not a possibility, nor is it even desirable. Who is clamouring to dash off to these meetings? That is what the voters elect and pay the politicians to do and pay the public servants to do. The only realistic avenue of participation is indirect, and here there is room for discussion. As things stand now, the public is represented in intergovernmental affairs by a narrow slice of the elected politicians, namely, the leaders of the governing parties at the federal, provincial, and territorial levels – the executives. This is indirect participation. Further, some members of the public are represented by whichever interest groups are involved in intergovernmental processes from time to time. While not at the table themselves, such groups – be they business organizations, environmental associations, professional associations, and so on – can lobby the officials who are. Indeed, interest groups are often consulted early on in the policy-development process and can find themselves closely involved in it at all stages.

While the public can be said to participate indirectly in the intergovernmental arena in the ways just described, no one would conclude that this amounts to a robust tradition of democratic participation. Even when the role of the interest groups is counted, the exercise has a behind-the-scenes quality that precludes widespread and informed public debate about whatever is at issue. Since there is little opportunity for public debate during the process, the only possibility is at the conclusion, when the political leaders have reached agreement on an issue. But this is when the absence of accountability mechanisms exacts a price. The political leaders do not need to bring the agreement back to their respective legislatures for a vote on it. The dispute-settlement mechanism and the national health council mentioned above are perfect examples.

As opinion polls continue to demonstrate, Canadians are vitally interested in health care. That being so, these could obviously be significant developments that would directly affect the service they receive. Why? Consider the dispute-settlement mechanism. Prior to its adoption, the federal government could withhold revenues from any province that it suspected of compromising the standards set out in the Canada Health Act. Now it has agreed to a process that requires it to refer any such dispute to a three-member panel that will serve as a referee between the two sides. If it gets off the ground, the new process may or may not turn out to be a good thing. Some health activists regard it as a bad thing that will undermine the federal government's capacity to enforce the federal standards. The important point here is that neither the federal leaders nor the provincial leaders had to subject the dispute-settlement mechanism to a debate and a vote in their respective legislatures. This fact, whatever the issue, has the effect of keeping such issues off the political agenda. While nothing prevents the opposition parties from addressing an issue, it is much easier for them to do so when it is scheduled for debate in the legislature. In any event, what is the point of addressing an issue that is a fait accompli, and not put to a vote?

Moreover, there is the fact that habits develop. In the parliamentary system, the key process for publicizing an issue is the debate between the governing party and the opposition party or parties. When the two sides join in debate about something, the media have a product that they can dramatize and disseminate to the public at large. The opposition has long since become used to the idea that the arena of executive federalism tends not to produce debatable outcomes, except for constitutional proposals, which are always potentially explosive. Instead executive federalism tends to produce done deals. To reiterate, there is no process under which the political leaders need to return to their respective legislatures to consult them before signing on the dotted line. So that opportunity for public debate is foregone, and along with it the unpredictability that is a key condition of public interest and participation in the political process. And so it goes. The closed processes of executive federalism can have the effect of immunizing controversies between the two levels of government from public debate, because the legislatures are excluded from these processes.

Conclusion

The federal system at the same time enhances and discourages democratic participation in political life, which seems something of a paradox. The system encourages democratic participation because it breaks up the governing structures into manageable components, each with some important public business to transact. Citizens can engage governments at the national, provincial, territorial, and local levels. Naturally those who want to influence the conduct of the country's foreign policy face a much tougher challenge than those who are pursuing their local councillor for road repairs. Nevertheless, opportunities for civic engagement exist at the different governmental levels of the system. It is not a monolith.

Of course the system's very complexity also exacts transaction costs. Those who want to participate in the development of public policy need to figure out which level of government does what, be prepared to face daunting organizational problems should they plan to associate with others across the country, and deploy time and financial resources in their participatory efforts. Given the nature of the federal system, much of this seems unavoidable, although aficionados of Internet communications claim to see possibilities of democratic participation in the use of such technology.

Then there is the practice of executive federalism, under which governments deal with one another as executives, which practice has the effect of closing the proceedings to all but the invited. This lesson of executive federalism was never lost on Aboriginal leaders. The Constitution Act, 1982 contains provisions that recognize the rights of Aboriginal peoples. Once those provisions were in place, Aboriginal leaders pressed harder than ever their demand to be present at conferences of the federal and provincial governments, especially but not exclusively the constitutional conferences. They know how important it is to be at the table – as leaders of territorially based governments – when the issues are debated and sometimes determined.

Paradoxically the very practice that normally closes out the public occasionally lets them in. When there is sharp, deep conflict between the governments the public gets to see through the cracks. This goes to the third test of the audit, the responsiveness of the federal system to Canadians, which is the subject of the next chapter.

CHAPTER 5

- Executive federalism has echoes of international relations.
- Governmental elites dominate decision making.
- The agreements negotiated by government leaders are often presented to the public as "done deals."
- Executive federalism blurs the lines of political accountability of governments to legislatures.
- Executive federalism is more functional than democratic.

DEMOCRATIC AUDIT OF RESPONSIVENESS IN THE FEDERAL SYSTEM

6

It can be stated that inclusion is a condition of participation, which in turn is a condition of responsiveness. Certainly the statement has an easy, logical ring to it. Yet responsiveness involves more than inclusion and participation. Citizens who are included in the political system and choose to participate actively in it are not thereby guaranteed a government that is responsive to their particular concerns. Responsiveness must be exacted by some mechanism or other. The principal mechanism is the election.

Governments are made responsive to citizens by being made accountable to them. In democratic systems, federal or otherwise, the key engine of accountability is still the election that is held at regular, or at least relatively regular, intervals. Knowing that they can be thrown out of office, elected officials have a strong incentive to respond to the demands of the electorate or at least to be seen as responding to them.

The election is certainly a powerful engine of accountability. It is so powerful, and highly regarded, that the worst autocrats expend considerable energy staging their own elections so that they look better in the eyes of the world, if not in the eyes of their weary citizens, who know better. To the autocrats, even a fake election is better than no election. But a fake election is nothing like a real election. Real elections are competitive occasions on which the voters have rival candidates and political parties to choose among. At issue in this chapter is how the federal system affects the competitive quality of elections at the national, provincial, and local levels.

There is also responsiveness between elections, or the extent to which governments appear to be responding to the ongoing concerns of individual citizens, organizations, and interest groups when no electoral outing is on the immediate horizon. This too can usefully be regarded as a matter of competitiveness. There need to be built-in public critics of the government, as it were, as well as built-in sources of alternative policy proposals. Individuals and organized groups may or may not be successful in getting governments to respond to them. Whatever the case, responsiveness cannot be measured by their fate, since no government will wish to or promise to or even ought to respond to all of the pressures exerted on it. Still, elected governments operate within a climate of public opinion to which they are often necessarily quite sensitive. And built-in or institutionalized centres of opposition are an important component of that climate because they reliably help to educate public opinion. At issue here is the relationship between the federal system and the centres of opposition – the checks and balances – that are so critical to the responsiveness of the governments between elections.

Federalism and the Competitiveness of Elections

Elections are held at all levels of government, but not at the same time, or even at predictable times. The national and provincial governments and two of the territorial governments are parliamentary, responsible governments in which the governing party has some leeway in deciding exactly when to call an election within a period of five years from the previous one. An exception is British Columbia, which has legislated a four-year term. For the rest, ordinarily the government will choose a time favourable to its own chances at the polls. Occasionally a governing party loses the confidence of the legislature, and for that reason is forced into an election unexpectedly, which can still happen in BC before the four years are finished. By contrast, municipal elections generally are held at regular three-year intervals. In any event, the federal system entails lots of elections. If that alone spelled responsiveness, then federalism would be a hands-down democratic winner. But elections in and of themselves do not spell responsiveness; instead their competitive quality does. In order to judge competitiveness, some brief comments are necessary about the electoral system and political parties.

As noted earlier, Canadian elections mostly use the first-past-the-post system, more formally referred to as the single-member plurality (SMP) system, and have done since Confederation. Candidates run in geographically defined electoral districts, and the winner is the one with the most votes. In many municipal elections the candidates for mayor or warden and the candidates for election to the council run as individuals rather than as members of a political party. In the parliamentary systems at the federal, provincial, and territorial levels, however, the political parties dominate: the serious candidates for office are the candidates of the political parties. The competitiveness of the electoral system thus depends upon the competitiveness of the party system.

In fact, the political party system in Canada is not widely regarded as robustly competitive (see Cross 2004). On the contrary, at different times and at different levels of government, the system has been notably uncompetitive, featuring one party in office for long periods and weak opposition parties. Some quick examples will illustrate the phenomenon that political scientists call "one-party dominance." At the federal level, in the nineteenth century the Conservative Party held office from 1878 to 1896, at which point the Liberal Party gained office and held it until 1911. The longest tenure was still to come — twenty-two years of Liberal governments from 1935 to 1957. A similar pattern can be found at the provincial level, with one party holding office for long periods of time. The hands-down winner is the Social

Credit Party of Alberta, which won office in 1935 and did not relinquish it until 1971 – a solid thirty-six years.

The length of tenure of the governing party is not the only signal of an uncompetive party system. Another is the size of the governing party's majority in the legislature. On more than one occasion in the provinces, the winning party has taken all of the seats in the legislature – all of them! When this happened in PEI in 1935, the event was held to be the first of its kind in any Commonwealth country as well as a blow to democracy, since the Liberal Party accomplished the feat on the basis of 58 percent of the popular vote. The opposition Conservatives got nothing for their share of vote, which was just over 40 percent. Landslides just short of this magnitude have peppered the Island's landscape ever since, the most recent in 1989 and 1993, when the opposition was reduced to two members and one member, respectively. In the New Brunswick election in 1987, the Liberal Party led by the popular Frank McKenna routed the Progressive Conservative government of Premier Richard Hatfield – not a single PC candidate was elected to the legislature. These were extraordinarily lopsided victories in which majorities in the popular vote were translated into total victories in the legislature, with no opposition voices there at all. Such a ridiculous result is an extreme example of a third indicator of an uncompetive party system: a weak opposition.

The opposition can be weak short of complete annihilation. For example, the leading opposition party might have one-third or fewer of the seats in the legislature, and therefore find itself with too few members to mount an effective attack against the government, serve on legislative committees, and maintain the pace of debate in the legislature. Many years ago political scientist Alan Cairns (1968, 58) made the suggestion that the one-third level is the minimum for an effective opposition, although, as he conceded, it is an arbitrary figure. However, the number of opposition parties can also make for an ineffective opposition.

In a two-party system, there is one opposition party which, all other things being equal, is able to mount a coherent and organized attack against the government's policies. If there is more than one party in opposition, this strength is lost. Several parties mount attacks against the government from different political positions – a cacophony of voices rather than a sustained assault. Moreover, opposition parties cannot be expected to work easily together; often they are as opposed to one another as they are to the government. The weakness of the multiparty opposition has been on display at the federal level in Canada since the Liberals returned to office in 1993, having been out of office since 1984. In the wake of the 1993 general election, four parties faced the governing Liberals: the Bloc Québécois, the Reform Party, the Progressive Conservatives, and the New Democratic Party. After the general election in 2000, the same four parties were in opposition, the Reform Party having become the Canadian Alliance party. Throughout this period it has been commonly observed that the governing Liberals led by Prime Minister Jean Chrétien have had the benefit of weak opposition parties that have been unable to cause them any real trouble with the voters.

Importantly, the issue here is the weakness of the institutionalized opposition. In parliamentary systems, the opposition to the government is said to be institutionalized because it is built into the system in the form of Her Majesty's Loyal Opposition. However arcane the phraseology, it expresses the important principle that citizens who criticize the government are still loyal citizens. Further, it conveys the idea that there is a known, public centre of opposition to the government around which critics can flock. This is why it is troubling to find that the institutionalized opposition is often weak – weak in numbers and weak in its capacity to act as the chief critic of the government. Moreover, in a parliamentary system weakness feeds on weakness. Typically the resources available to the government overwhelm the resources available to the opposition. The government has the expertise of the public service at its disposal. It also has the capacity to make appointments and authorize contracts, both of which can be used, frankly, to reward its supporters. The opposition has none of these opportunities.

Another point, blindingly obvious but still worth noting about both levels of government, is that the system contains no other institutionalized site of opposition. The opposition sits in the legislature, across the aisle from the government. Theoretically the Senate could serve as a site of opposition within the system at the federal level, but it is not constituted to do that. And none of the provinces has a senate or upper house; they all have unicameral or one-house legislatures. It is possible, of course, to include a second site of opposition in the design of the parliamentary system. In Australia, for example, the Commonwealth government (the central government) includes an elected Senate in which effective opposition to the government can be mobilized.

The electoral system is without doubt a main reason why the political-party system is not as competitive as it might be. It has been demonstrated that in Canada's multiparty system, the SMP system rarely translates accurately a party's percentage of votes received (say 20 percent) into the same percentage of seats in the legislature (20 percent). Instead there is a pattern of inaccurate translation. Usually the leading party gets a greater percentage of seats in the legislature than the percentage of votes received. As a result, its presence in the legislature is enhanced. Meanwhile, the second party often gets a smaller percentage of seats in the legislature than the percentage of votes received, so its presence in the legislature is diminished. By contrast, smaller parties with votes concentrated in a region sometimes get more seats than votes, and therefore gain weight in the legislature out of proportion to their level of public support.

Overall, then, the electoral system helps to produce a weaker opposition than the votes cast in an election would indicate ought to be the case. A quick example will help make the point. In the 2000 federal election, the Liberal Party won 41 percent of the votes cast and 52 percent of the seats in the House of Commons. In other words, with only a plurality of votes the party gained a majority of the seats, a very efficient result indeed. The Bloc also did well, getting 13 percent of the seats with 11 percent of the votes. The Alliance got 22 percent of the seats with a 22 percent vote share. On the other hand, the NDP and the

PC Party, both of which have support across the country, achieved the reverse result. The NDP got 4 percent of the seats with its 9 percent vote share; and the PCs got 4 percent of the seats with 12 percent of the votes, the worst result of all.

However important the electoral system, the background factor of federalism must still be taken into account. The combination of federalism and the SMP electoral system has encouraged the development of a multiparty system in which different parties are competitive in different regions, and no two parties are competitive at any one time across the country. Federalism is a contributing factor because it defines and accentuates the differences among the regions of the country. Almost by definition federalism has the effect of accentuating regionalism. It provides a context in which parties that appeal to regional interests can thrive. But while they can thrive, they find it hard to overcome the very regionalism that gave them a start in the first place so as to become national organizations capable of making a national appeal. The Western-based Reform Party and its successor, the Canadian Alliance, are instructive examples.

The Reform Party was established in 1987 in the midst of the constitutional round that featured the Meech Lake Accord, a document largely designed to meet the concerns of Quebec about its status and powers within the federation. According to the party's first and only leader, Preston Manning (1992, v), its founders were motivated by "a feeling of being left out of our own country." They felt alienated, a phenomenon so widespread that it is often referred to simply as Western alienation. Their complaint was that the federal government consistently gave priority to Quebec over the West on constitutional issues (Meech Lake) and to southern Ontario over the West on economic issues (the National Energy Program, widely perceived in the West to penalize western resource producers in order to subsidize eastern energy consumers). The Reform Party's plan was to promote some reforms of the federal system that would have the effect of better representing and therefore elevating the concerns of the West within the system. The "Triple-E Senate" – equal, effective, elected – became one of its better-known proposals.

While the Reform Party had some success in the elections of 1993 and especially 1997, when it assumed the role of the official Opposition, it was never able to break out of its electoral base, which remained largely confined to Alberta and BC. In particular, the party did not poll well in Ontario, a critical weakness since it could never hope to poll well in Quebec, the concerns of which province it showed little capacity to comprehend or want to meet. In 1998 Manning launched an effort to transform the party from a vehicle of regional protest to a national party. The result was the Canadian Alliance, which contested the 2000 election under a new leader, Stockwell Day. The results were disappointing for the Alliance, which was unable to make the breakthrough in other regions that it had sought. The party was unable to "unite the right," as was said at the time (Mendelsohn 2002, 62-4). Although there are lots of conservative-minded voters across the country, in the east many of them were still attached to the traditional party of conservatives, the Progressive Conservative Party, the lineage of which stretched back to Confederation.

In the years following the election, support for a union of the two parties in their respective memberships grew along with the recognition that, separately, neither could complete with the governing Liberal Party. Eventually the leaders of the two parties entered into merger talks that culminated in a proposal to establish a new party, the Conservative Party. In a vote held in December 2003, the memberships gave the proposal overwhelming support. The following March the new party chose its new leader, Stephen Harper. In the meantime the Alliance remains a classic example of a regional party in a federal system that was unable to put together a national coalition sufficiently robust to challenge the governing party. Then there is the Bloc Québécois, another product of the unsuccessful Meech Lake Accord. Upset by the demise of the accord, which demise he interpreted to be a signal failure of Canadian federalism to accommodate the uniqueness of Quebec, Lucien Bouchard, one of the leading cabinet ministers from the province, left the government and founded the Bloc Québécois. The Bloc won so many seats in Quebec in the 1993 election that it edged out the Reform Party to become the official

Opposition. The Bloc's status in the House was ironic, to say the least, since the purpose of the party is to accelerate the independence of Quebec rather than to govern the country. It is a truly regional party.

As a result of such factors as the federal system and the SMP electoral system, then, Canada has developed a multiparty system that enables a governing party to capture a majority of the seats in the House of Commons on the basis of the support of a minority of the electorate. Such a government could hardly be as responsive to the electorate as it would if it had to get majority support there. A coalition government made up of more than one party might have the support of a majority of the electorate, thereby injecting more democratic responsiveness into the system. But Canada has no tradition of coalition governments. On the contrary, there has been a flat rejection of the idea. It has to be concluded that elections, the chief mechanism by which governments are made responsive to the electorate, are not always sufficiently competitive to exact as much responsiveness as might be expected. And the federal system is part of the problem to the extent that it affects the capacity of the political parties to compete across the country. However, elections are not the only mechanism of responsiveness. During the period between elections, other mechanisms are – or should be – in place.

Federalism and Competitiveness between Elections

The governing party with a majority of the seats in the legislature can count on an easy ride there so long as its members remain loyal, which they do, Canadian parliamentary parties being among the most disciplined to be found in any parliamentary system. Nor is there an elected Senate of whom the government needs to be solicitous between elections. Is there anything at all? Well, yes, there are the provincial governments. They are a guaranteed, built-in, institutionalized opposition to the federal government. At all times, too, since at any given moment at least one of the ten, if not more, is bound to be at odds with the federal government about something, and not loath to make the point in public.

It must be stressed that nothing in the Constitution directly or expressly gives the provinces such a role. They fall into this opposition role as a by-product of the federal system that is mandated under the Constitution. Competition between the two levels of government is more or less ensured by the federal principle of the division of powers, under which each level possesses exclusive power to act within the policy areas assigned to it. Each level is empowered to act independently of the other within its assigned areas. But because policies made in one area are bound to affect policies in another area, which is known as policy interdependence, it is impossible for the two levels to act in splendid isolation from one another. For example, the provinces are assigned exclusive jurisdiction in education. The policies that they adopt in education, however, affect more than the educational institutions, the professionals who work in them, and the students. They also affect the job market and ultimately the competitiveness of the economy as a whole. Understandably the federal government is interested in what the provinces are doing in education.

Given the reality of policy interdependence, governments can and do collide. In the collision lies the competition between them. And what are they competing for? Ultimately, for votes. Being elected, the governments always maintain a watchful eye on the voters. They do not want to find themselves on the wrong side of the voters on an issue of importance to them. In the normal course of events, this is not a huge concern. Voters are divided on the issues of the day in terms of both their positions on the issues and their level of interest in them, which sometimes amounts to no interest at all. Further, even when an issue is important to voters, they might not care to sort out which level of government is actually the policy maker. On the other hand, voters might be well aware of which government is on which side, either because it is clear, or because one or both of the governments wants to make it clear. In such situations the governments are competing with one another for the support of the respective electorates. This competition has the effect of cracking open the debate

and letting the citizens in. It exposes the issues and the policy alter-
natives, and demonstrates to the citizens that there are choices to be
made – choices that will be made. An excellent example is the Kyoto
Protocol.

Kyoto: High Tension in Intergovernmental Relations

The Kyoto Protocol, which flows from the United Nations Framework
Convention on Climate Change, addresses the problem of global
warming. It was signed in Kyoto, Japan, in 1997 by representatives of
countries around the world, including Canada. Under the protocol,
the industrialized countries are required by the period from 2008 to
2012 to cut the emission of the greenhouse gases that are generated
by burning fossil fuels to levels below 1990 levels. The protocol is
driven by the concern that unchecked, rising levels of greenhouse
gases will trigger environmental disasters.

It was one thing for the federal government to sign the protocol at
Kyoto. It was quite another thing to ratify it, since ratification is a
commitment to implement the protocol, that is, to reduce the emission of greenhouse gases, which is a costly endeavour. Fossil fuels
like coal, gasoline, and oil are used extensively in the industrialized
world. Since the day the protocol was signed, and in anticipation of
its likely costs to their economies, the industrialized countries have
been busy seeking creative ways to meet emissions targets, not simply by reducing emissions across the board but also by using market
mechanisms that would allow them to purchase emission reductions
in return for the use of clean energy and for making investments in
developing countries. The purpose of these market mechanisms obviously is to limit the actual emission reductions that a country needs
to make.

As a result of the development of these emission strategies – cyn-
ics call them avoidance strategies – in June 2002 the federal government signalled its desire to ratify the protocol by the end of the year,

but not before completing an extensive process of consultation on the terms of ratification with the provincial and territorial governments, stakeholders, and other Canadians. The stakeholders included environmental organizations, which invariably supported the Kyoto commitment, and business interests, most but not all of which opposed it.

In promising an extensive consultation process before ratifying the agreement, the federal government appeared to be following the path required by the federal system. (Eventually it rescinded that decision, about which more later.) First it is worth considering exactly why the federal system seems to compel elaborate consultations with the provinces on an issue of this kind. The answer is the Constitution. Given the enormous implications of the Kyoto Protocol for the economy – mostly negative, incidentally – consultation with industry as well as other groups was essential. But the key to the success of the consultations was the provinces, because Kyoto is about environmental protection. The constitutional division of powers, being a nineteenth-century construct, makes no mention of the environment. As a result, legislative responsibility for the environment flows from other responsibilities assigned to the federal and provincial governments, making the environment a concurrent or shared jurisdiction. The provincial position is derived from jurisdiction over natural resources, municipal institutions, and "matters of a local and private nature" within the province. The federal position is derived from jurisdiction over interprovincial and international trade, the seacoasts and the fisheries off them, and Parliament's general power to legislate for the "peace, order, and good government" of the country. Latterly the Supreme Court of Canada has strengthened the federal government's hand in the area (Baier 2002, 28-30). Nevertheless, the environment is very much a shared jurisdiction, and therefore successful policy initiatives of any significance arguably require the collaboration of the governments.

To date, the most important product of such collaboration is the Canada-Wide Accord on Environmental Harmonization and accompanying subagreements, signed in 1998 by the federal, provincial, and territorial environment ministers, excepting Quebec, which declined to sign the accord. Among the objectives of the accord are the development of consensus-based decisions on national standards of environmental protection and procedures to identify which level of government deals with which sort of environmental issue. The federal government initially sought to pursue the same collaborative approach to the implementation of the Kyoto agreement. But Kyoto is an international agreement, which gives the provinces another leg to stand on in addition to the fact that the environment is a shared responsibility.

Under the Constitution, the federal government has the power to make treaties with the governments of other countries. This is the treaty-making power. Unless treaties are given effect, however, they are worthless. Under the Constitution, should the subject matter of the treaty involve a provincial policy area, then it is for the provinces to implement the treaty – or not. In other words, the federal government cannot guarantee the implementation of a treaty on a provincial matter unless it has the agreement of the provinces. Thus it would appear that the federal government needed the agreement of the provinces to honour its commitment to the Kyoto Protocol. The trouble is that one province was offside – very offside.

Given the importance of the fossil fuel industries to the economy of Alberta, it is no surprise that the province was on the warpath. Alberta argued that its economy would suffer the most in the implementation of Kyoto. And it had a point. In May 2002 the federal government released a discussion paper outlining options for cutting greenhouse gases to meet the Kyoto targets. The cheapest option was to impose an overall cap on emissions and require the industries that produce them to enter an emissions-trading system in which they could buy and sell emissions credits. This would place the heaviest burden on Alberta, which has a disproportionate share of such industries. The most expensive option – which spreads the burden more evenly – involved massive public investments in urban transit, clean and renewable energy sources, and clean-energy projects in developing countries. The remaining options were combinations of these two (Canada.comNews 2002, 1).

In the meantime, Alberta generated a rival plan that was focused entirely on making cuts in emissions in Canada, extended the target date for doing so to 2020, and proposed reductions in particular gases like carbon dioxide rather than the overall reductions specified under the Kyoto Protocol. A main assumption behind the plan was that new and better ways of cutting emissions were bound to be developed during the longer period. At a meeting of energy and environment ministers held in Charlottetown in May 2002, Alberta sought to have its plan added to the other options that the federal government was scheduled to present to the public in a consultative process designed to produce a national consensus on a strategy to implement the protocol. The province was unsuccessful in getting its plan formally denoted as a fifth option. However, at the meeting it was agreed that the provinces and the territories would decide for themselves whether to include Alberta's plan in any upcoming public hearings that met in their jurisdictions. As might be expected, Alberta lobbied the provinces and the territories to do just that at the venue of the annual Western Premiers' Conference, held in early June in Dawson City, Yukon. The result was inconclusive, but the forum itself was a sympathetic one in which the Alberta premier could fully present the province's case. And Alberta's actions had some effect elsewhere, an example being the Federation of Canadian Municipalities, convening at its annual meeting in early June. Although the Federation threw its support behind Kyoto, in response to the arguments made by Alberta's municipal leaders it added a couple of caveats to the effect that emissions from natural gas and electricity ought to be the responsibility of the consuming rather than the producing region and that no region of the country should bear the brunt of the emissions reductions (Pedersen 2002, 1).

As the account thus far is meant to suggest, the politics of executive federalism, supplemented by the odd opinion poll, which at that point indicated a majority of Canadians supported Kyoto, were proceeding apace. The offside province, Alberta, working within governmental circles, lobbied hard to prevent the federal government from ratifying the protocol, and certainly not before reaching an implementation plan agreeable to the province. Then in September 2002, Prime Minister Chrétien attended an environmental summit in Johannesburg, South Africa, and there announced that Canada would ratify the Kyoto Protocol by the end of the year, period – presumably no matter what happened in any consultation process. The announcement was a bombshell; even members of the federal cabinet appeared unprepared for it. The Alberta government was apoplectic. Premier Ralph Klein immediately called on the prime minister to convene a conference of first ministers or be prepared to face a major showdown with the anti-Kyoto provinces. Then he established a blue-ribbon committee of Albertans led by former premier Peter Lougheed, which was charged with advising the government on the best way to oppose the protocol.

On the advice of the committee, Alberta pursued a number of strategies, among them a campaign to educate the public on the consequences of ratifying Kyoto for the province's economy, stressing foregone investment by the oil and gas industry, the loss of tax revenues, and the loss of jobs. The province worked hard to convince other provincial governments, in particular Ontario's, to join it in opposing ratification. Finally it continued to flog its own plan for reducing greenhouse-gas emissions as a balanced alternative to Kyoto – slower but less of a threat to economic growth. Just having a plan was an advantage so long as Ottawa was without one. Since announcing its intention to ratify Kyoto in South Africa, Ottawa had stalled on the production of a plan to show how the Kyoto standards would be met within the Kyoto time frame, largely because Alberta had managed effectively to mobilize the business-sector opponents of Kyoto. By the end of October, however, Ottawa had produced a draft proposal of the emissions cuts to be made by individual Canadians and by industry, stressing that it was merely a "rough" draft and therefore subject to negotiation among the federal and provincial political leaders (Chase 2002). And the politics continued.

Although there was no need to do so under the terms of the Constitution, the federal government had decided to ask Parliament to express its opinion on the Kyoto Protocol through a vote. Public opinion polls continued to show that a majority of Canadians – decreasing by the day but still a majority – favoured the protocol. And the government could count on the support of a majority in the legislature. A successful vote would help to legitimate the government's position on Kyoto. At the same time, Alberta's opposition to the protocol had galvanized both the Alliance and the Conservatives, both of which shared the province's concerns and articulated them effectively in the debate on ratification that began in the last week of November. Although the vote was a foregone conclusion, the debate was informed and an educative exercise from the standpoint of the attentive public.

While the debate in Parliament was still under way, the federal government released its implementation plan. The key elements of the plan indicate that Alberta's campaign was not without effect. The federal government is consulting with the large industrial emitters on the establishment of their emission-reduction targets. Moreover, the government is making money available to them as they undertake the transition to the technologies needed to meet the targets. Commenting on this, one columnist wrote: "Let's call it on Kyoto: The oil industry won, as it usually does" (Reguly 2002). He could have written that Alberta won, too. The federal government's plan, by the way, is just as easy on consumers, since they are only asked to reduce their own greenhouse-gas emissions rather than being required to do so.

In mid-December, the House of Commons ended debate on the ratification of the protocol and voted in favour of it. The prime minister signed the protocol and sent it to the United Nations along with the environment minister, who presented it to the international organization in a nice little ceremony. Back home, in a fitting dénouement for this phase of things and an indication of what lies ahead, the Alliance critic of the environment ministry steamed, "We will be watching this government at every budget to examine how much it wastes chasing this potential economic disaster" (Dunfield 2002). What he and any other interested observer have seen in the months since is the federal government's efforts to reassure the petroleum producers that Kyoto will not reduce the competitiveness of their industry (Canada 2003, 6).

The Kyoto episode was high-level conflict in the politics of executive federalism. It was showy stuff, but what does it say about the role of federalism in the responsiveness of governments to the electorate? The first thing it says is that a provincial government can be an effective centre of opposition to the federal government, even when the federal government has the support of the other provincial and territorial governments. The Alberta government advanced the views of important industry opponents of the Kyoto Protocol within and without the province, and by extension all other opponents of it. Moreover, in the realization that the federal government was bent on ratifying Kyoto, Alberta put forward an alternative plan. This plan provoked debate, more debate than might otherwise have taken place, and at the start of the public consultation process. And ultimately the province extracted from the federal government an implementation plan that seems designed to ensure that the country as a whole shoulders the burden of the Kyoto commitment, and not mainly the oil and gas sector in Alberta.

Clearly, then, the actions of the Alberta government injected into the process the competitive element that is required to trigger democratic responsiveness. The provincial government is acutely attuned to the province's electorate. It is well aware of the widespread concern of Albertans for the economic consequences of the implementation of the protocol and their clear understanding that Alberta has more at stake than provinces that rely on clean – or cleaner – energy sources like hydroelectricity. The federal government can be assumed to be equally aware of these things and not bent on compelling the province to assume the heaviest burden in implementing the protocol. Even though the current federal government is not strong in electoral terms in Alberta, it has no reason to alienate the voters there gratuitously.

In the clash with the Alberta government, however, the federal government was bound to be made more responsive to the province's concerns in its handling of the situation. Moreover, Alberta's opposition revivified opposition to Kyoto in the House of Commons. There the chief opposition party, the Alliance, led the charge against the government on Alberta's behalf. Given the Alliance Party's roots in Alberta, this is hardly a surprise. For our purposes, the important point is that in the course of debating Kyoto, the party raised all kinds of issues about the protocol and its consequences for the economy that the ordinary citizen initially might not have considered.

The Kyoto case is an illuminating example of governments engaged in consultation on a critical, national issue between elections. The implementation of the Kyoto Protocol stands to affect everyone in the country – or at least their pocketbooks. Therefore the federal government needs to generate a consensus on implementation. Even if the public consultation process had taken place as planned initially, that is, in advance of the federal government's decision to ratify Kyoto, it is worth asking, who is the public? Most Canadians would not have attended any meetings. Even if they knew a little about the issue, they would expect the governments to represent their interests. Further, the federal government in particular can be expected to pursue a consensus, and in that pursuit not to welcome criticism but to marginalize it. A consensus is not unanimity, but even a consensus requires that some points of view be deflected – or better still ignored altogether.

Nevertheless, the system is a federal system. And the government of the province in which is located many of the chief sinners (from the standpoint of the advocates of the Kyoto Protocol) had the opportunity under the system to make itself a centre of opposition to the federal government. In availing itself of this opportunity, the Alberta government forced the debate over Kyoto into the open and onto the front pages of the newspapers. It focused the debate on the cost of implementing the protocol to the average Canadian. Ultimately it is the structure of federalism that permitted Alberta to do this. Federalism

– not the federal government or the advocates of the Kyoto Protocol or the political parties – generated the competitive environment that is so necessary for a responsive democracy (Tanguay 2002).

Conclusion

In terms of the responsiveness of governments, secured at elections and between elections, federalism is a saw-off. On the one hand, the federal system undoubtedly serves to accentuate the regionalism that is such a difficult obstacle to a competitive national party system. At any one time, there seem never to be two national parties that compete with one another in federal elections. Usually there is only the winning party, which can make some claim to have national support, and the rest. The rest are incredibly weak parties with national aspirations, and regionally based parties. The result is a governing party that gains more electoral success than is warranted by its actual level of support among the electorate, which circumstance is hardly a guarantee of democratic responsiveness. On the other hand, between elections the federal structure sets the stage for a competitive dynamic between the federal government and the provinces that helps to strengthen the responsiveness of the system to citizens.

The competitive dynamic is between elites, of course. The general public mostly can only watch the action from the bleachers rather than getting directly involved. But public opinion is an important factor in these contests. The governments polled Canadians about Kyoto on an ongoing basis, and each side claimed to have public opinion in its camp. On the basis of its polling early on, the federal government found Canadians generally in support of ratification of the protocol, including Albertans. For its part, the Alberta government found that the more people learned about the protocol, the less they were inclined to favour it. Soon opinion in the province swung to the provincial government's side. So the competition between the governments to some extent engaged the public in the issue, or rather the publics, since the federal government polled nationally and the Alberta government polled provincially. This was exactly the kind of competition that Breton (1985) had in mind when he extolled the benefits of classical federalism.

Let us recall his argument, set out in Chapter 2, to the effect that under the classical structure, independently empowered governments can find themselves in competition for the support of their respective publics, and when they do the result is to enhance the openness and responsiveness of the system as a whole. The competition secures the democracy. By contrast, when the division of powers between the two levels of government is muddied and there is governmental collaboration instead of competition, then the competitive dynamic is lost, and democracy is the loser. But what is the cost of competition?

However persuasive the Breton analysis might appear in the light of the Kyoto example, the matter cannot be left there. Competition has a price, too. It is important to appreciate that Kyoto, unhappily, resurrects the prototypical divide between Alberta and the federal government. Once again the two are at odds over a major energy issue. In the background is the bitter memory of the dust-up between the two governments over the federal government's National Energy Program (NEP), which was an attempt to enlarge the role of the state in the energy sector in an effort to ensure that the country controlled its own energy supply. The NEP was a response to the successful effort of the world's largest producers of oil, the Arab countries, to organize a cartel of oil-producing nations to control production and thereby maintain what they regarded as a reasonable price for the product. Alberta reacted very strongly against the NEP, which was regarded as an unreasonable and costly (to Alberta) intrusion into the energy sector on the part of the federal government. And in the event the NEP did do damage to Alberta's economy, damage from which it took many years to recover. Lougheed, the head of the advisory committee on Kyoto, is not simply a former premier of Alberta but the premier at the time of the battle over the NEP, and he was quoted calling the Kyoto episode a "flashback" (Chase, Mackie, and Brethour 2002).

The point to be made is that the politics of executive federalism, while forcing debate into the open for all the world to see, do not necessarily lead to a consensus or a happy deal among the parties. Instead such politics can focus division, sharpen division, and embitter it. Such a result is particularly threatening to federal systems, which are always vulnerable to internal dissension that threatens the integrity of the country's boundaries − in other words, vulnerable to secession.

CHAPTER 6

- ⚲ In democratic systems the key engine of accountability is the election, which is held at regular intervals.

- ⚲ In Canada, the federal system and the SMP electoral system have combined to produce a multiparty system that includes regional parties.

- ⚲ The same combination of federal and SMP electoral systems makes it difficult for any one party to elect MPs from all regions of the country.

- ⚲ Canada has no tradition of coalition governments.

THE DEMOCRATIC AUDIT AND CHANGE IN THE FEDERAL SYSTEM

7

The democratic audit hinges on the criteria of inclusiveness, participation, and responsiveness. As the analysis that has unfolded in the preceding chapters reveals, the federal system has an impact on each of these three criteria.

On the criterion of inclusiveness, federalism privileges the territorial organization of political and governmental life, and not just any territorial organization. Specifically, it privileges the territorial organization that is mandated under the Constitution. Under the Canadian Constitution, the key territorially organized constituencies are the country, the provinces, and way behind them, the territories. Some of the territorially organized Aboriginal communities are gaining constitutional and political ground, although even the most advanced are not as close to self-governing status as they would like. The municipalities demarcate the contours of the local communities but as creatures of the provinces, the municipalities are neither secure in their boundaries nor securely possessed of their own particular set of powers. Non-territorially based communities are not recognized in this hierarchy of communities.

Inclusiveness governs participation. In a system of representative democracy, the key participants are the elected governments. In Canada the elected governments that matter are the governments of the territorial organizations that are mandated under the Constitution. First in line are the federal and provincial governments, followed by the rest, which have uneven claims. While territorially based Aboriginal communities have a foothold in the Constitution, for example, the municipalities have no such foothold there. Then there is the complicated situation of the territories. On the one hand they are the creatures of the federal government and can be made, unmade, or shifted around. On the other hand, the Aboriginal communities within them possess lands and self-governing rights in varying degrees. All is complexity. And yet the bottom line is that the territorially based governments are privileged by the design of the federal system and are the key players in it. These are the governments that the citizens elect and that they try to influence between elections. If the decision-making power within these governments is highly centralized, and if decision-making processes are closed rather than transparent, then the levels of citizen participation are bound to be lower than they would be if the reverse were true.

Canadians necessarily deal with multilevel governance. Thus an assessment of the criterion of responsiveness is an assessment of the responsiveness of the territorially based governments to the communities that elect them. The impact of federalism on responsiveness is partly a matter of the impact of executive federalism on responsiveness. As has been shown, executive federalism can often have the effect of shutting the citizens out of the processes of deliberation and decision making. Once governments reach a consensus on an issue, they present the public with what amounts to a fait accompli. When the issue proves highly divisive, however, the competitive interaction between the governments can help to open up the process to interested citizens and at the same time make the governments acutely responsive to the opinion of the respective publics that elect them.

The federal system obviously thus directly affects each of the criteria of the democratic audit. The question is whether it can be made to affect them in a more positive fashion. In other words, can it be made to enhance inclusiveness, participation, and responsiveness more than it does now? Is there a case for change? The short answer is yes. Before turning to the case for change, however, as well as to some specific changes that might be made, it is worth addressing the case against change. Even if this case is not compelling in reform-minded circles, at least it points to the need to be realistic about what can be accomplished in terms of democratic reforms to the structure of federalism.

The Case against Change

We saw the case against change in Chapter 2, in which Riker's argument (1964) that federalism is a bargain is set out. In Riker's view, federalism is not a bargain about democracy, but a bargain or compromise negotiated by the political leaders of the day, largely for military or economic reasons or both. The leaders could negotiate a union. But they stop short of a union, and instead negotiate a federal system because they do not want to unite. In other words, at the very core of the federal system is something slightly unstable. What happens if the reasons for the bargain disappear? What happens if one of the members becomes extremely unhappy with the system?

Confederation was a compromise struck in 1867. It was not a compromise negotiated by anyone and everyone. The elitist structures of the day more or less ensured that the governing economic and political classes alone were involved in the processes. The compromise was negotiated by the political leaders of the regions, which at the time were organized as British colonies and at Confederation morphed into the provinces.

It is probably fair to state that the compromise was fragile. In the early years, Confederation was maintained largely because the provincial governments were the key governments for most of the citizens. The federal government, far away in Ottawa, was not much involved in the lives of ordinary Canadians. When it was involved in important ways there was trouble. A good example in the nineteenth century is the National Policy (NP). In 1879 the federal government adopted a national economic policy that involved the establishment of high tariffs in order to nourish the infant manufacturing sector, and a transcontinental railway system in order to encourage east-west trade.

From the standpoint of central Canada, the NP was a wealth-generating success. From the standpoint of the Maritime provinces, then a resource-export region with a preference for low tariffs and not much of a manufacturing sector, the NP proved disastrous. It hobbled the export trade, decimated what little in the way of manu-facturing had been built up in connection with the export trade, and compelled the region to purchase goods expensively transported from central Canada, which was hundreds of miles away, rather than cheaper goods from the much closer New England states. One way or the other, the dollars wound up in central Canada. Understandably the NP caused ongoing political bickering between the region and Ottawa for decades, and eventually culminated in the Maritime Rights movement in the 1920s, which was an attempt to establish an effec-tive regional political voice in Ottawa, one that would transcend tra-ditional partisanship. Of course the movement collapsed and the region capitulated to its economic fate as a "have-not" region, a fate that persisted for decades but finally began to change for the better in the closing years of the twentieth century, Canada having adopted formally a free-trade economic regime with the United States in 1988.

The two world wars were occasions of strong federal leadership, when power was concentrated in Ottawa for the purpose of prosecut-ing the war effort. One result was a difficult relationship with Quebec. In the First World War, the relationship between the govern-ing Conservative Party and the province reached such a low following the dreadful election in 1917, which featured the issue of conscription in the armed services – the government imposed it against the oppo-sition of the Quebec government as well as individuals scattered throughout the country – that Conservative electoral prospects there faded for decades. Indeed, even now the party cannot be said to have recovered fully. Conscription was an issue again in the Second World War, although this time the governing Liberals under the wily Prime Minister Mackenzie King handled it more adroitly in the national referendum on conscription, as discussed in Chapter 5. The list hardly stops here. Other important public-policy initiatives taken by the federal government, such as the National Energy Program, also adverted to earlier, have been the cause of serious strain between it and a region. The most recent is the federal government's fisheries policy, particularly in the cod fishery. The government of Newfoundland and Labrador considers the policy a complete failure. The province is taking a tough line, among other things demanding a comanagement approach that would give it a greater role in the policy-making process than it has now.

These clashes over major national public policies emphasize the compromise inherent in the federal system. Arguably the compromise is as fragile as ever. Put differently, arguably the regionalism of the country is as strong as ever. Yet the compromise has endured, and that is a reason for being wary of change. Sometimes it is prudent to leave well enough alone. Change is not necessarily for the better. Moreover, a change made in the direction of democratizing the federal system such that the structure is made more inclusive, participatory, and responsive would not be a one-dimensional affair. Any one change is bound to have ramifications, possibly negative, for other aspects of the system. The federal system could be radically democratized and then fall apart. The trick is to know when doing nothing – making no change – is the greater danger.

The Case for Change: Inclusiveness

One episode in the Kyoto drama is an argument for strengthening the democratic credentials of the federal system. When the federal government released its implementation proposal in late October 2002 – the proposal being little more than a blueprint with few details – the

Quebec National Assembly voted unanimously to condemn it, complaining that the province was being asked to do more than its fair share under the proposal. The government demanded a separate, bilateral agreement with Ottawa based on the fact that the province uses "clean" hydroelectricity to fuel its economy, not dirty carbon fuels. It was the first province to make such a demand, and it did so before the consultations on the proposal had begun (Chase and Walton 2002).

There is nothing wrong in principle with a bilateral agreement: Ottawa signs all kinds of agreements with individual provinces. The point is that bilateralism was Quebec's instinctive reaction – a default position, no matter what is on the table. Even Alberta's proposed plan was meant for the country rather than simply for the province. The sense of inclusiveness in the federal system is not strong enough, it seems, to counteract the reflex action of a province-first position, especially but by no means exclusively on the part of Quebec. Quebec is the hard case, though, since its government has tried to lead it out of the federation. Quebec's position must be remembered when considering strengthening the federal system from the standpoint of the democratic criterion of inclusiveness.

On inclusiveness there are at least two directions to take, each of which has serious implications for the principal players in the system now, especially the provinces. One is to strengthen the extent to which Canadians are represented in the central government. This points directly to the Senate, since the Senate, being an appointed body, is the obvious target of democratic reform. The other direction is to widen the range of governments included in the processes of executive federalism. We begin here with the Senate, and deal with executive federalism in the next section.

INCLUSIVENESS AND A REFORMED SENATE

The chief way of enhancing inclusiveness in the federal government is to change the basis of the selection of members of the Senate from appointment by the prime minister to election. Obviously by definition election is a more democratic and therefore inclusive process than appointment, especially appointment by one person. Election is more inclusive from the standpoint of the voters; indeed, it is the only way that they can get involved in the selection of senators. The current system of appointment by the prime minister simply shuts voters out. Election is also likely to be more inclusive from the standpoint of the composition of the Senate. An elected Senate would likely represent a broader range of opinion from the provinces than it does now – elected opinion, not appointed opinion. There needs to be more room for elected officials from across the country to represent a range of points of view in the federal councils.

So far, so good. Now the hard part begins. No one who champions an elected Senate thinks that any old version will do (Smith 2003). On the contrary, a particular conception of what an elected Senate would look like and do almost always accompanies any particular reform proposal. Some want an elected Senate to strengthen the role of the provinces in the institutions of the central government; some want an elected Senate to produce the opposite effect, that is, to undermine the role of the provinces in the federation. Still others are not interested in the provinces at all, but instead see an elected Senate as an opportunity to represent Canadians in nonterritorial dimensions like gender, class, or ethnicity. Another possibility is an "independent" body, meaning independent of political parties. It is not enough, then, to suggest an elected Senate as a way to advance democratic inclusiveness in the system. Everything depends upon the type of system that is used to elect senators, as the following examples illustrate.

The best way to strengthen the role of the provinces in the central government is to establish a Senate whose members are elected by the provincial legislatures. This is indirect election. The senators are bound to be responsive to the provincial legislatures that elect them, legislatures that in turn are dominated by the provincial governments. The provincial governments would have reliable spokespersons for their position in the Senate.

By contrast, the best way to undermine the role of the provinces in the federation is to establish a Senate whose members are elected by the voters of each of the provinces. It is unlikely that provincial governments could control such elections. Instead they might well produce senators with views that are very different from those of the governments of the provinces in which they reside. Years ago political scientist Roger Gibbins (1982, 45-79; see also D.E. Smith 1995, 169) made this point, arguing that an elected Senate would compete with the provincial governments to represent opinion in the provinces on national issues. Unelected senators cannot make the claim that they represent provincial opinion on national issues for the simple reason that no one voted them into office to do that. As a result, provincial governments often take on that job, even though strictly speaking under the Constitution they represent the residents of the provinces for provincial purposes only. If the Senate were elected by provincial electorates, it could do the job of representing those electorates on national issues, thereby authoritatively feeding more voices into the national discourse and in the process strengthening the legitimacy of that discourse and, by extension, the central government itself.

Next are those who want to strengthen the representation of the nonterritorial (read nonprovincial) dimensions of political life. If the dimensions at issue are gender, class, or ethnicity, then the problem is rather difficult to solve. In addition to the distinction between indirect and direct election, there are the many forms of direct election, ranging from the single-member plurality system that Canada uses now to forms of proportional representation. (Courtney 2004 discusses the various electoral systems at length.) The key point is the problem of engineering an electoral system to produce the desired representational effect. For example, under a system of proportional representation, the political parties might be able to give more thought to including women and individuals from other underrepresented categories on their tickets. But it is also possible – in some provinces probable – that proportional representation would have the effect of encouraging new "province first" political parties to field candidates. Such political parties might do awfully well, and if so, the Senate would become the province-based body that the nonterritorialists hope not to see.

Finally there are those who would like to see a Senate with members who are independent of political parties. Certainly they see little point in generating an elected Senate that looks exactly like the House of Commons. An electoral system that encourages independents is not an easy thing to find. In Australia the Senate is elected on the basis of the single transferable vote, which is a proportional system used in multimember districts, that is, districts out of which more than one candidate is elected. In each district, the number of votes that the candidates need to win is set – the quota. The voters rank the candidates in order of preference. The next preferences of a candidate who achieves the quota and is named a winner are redistributed to the remaining candidates, a process that continues until the assigned number of members for the district is named. The single transferable vote is held to be more favourable to the prospects of independent candidates than most other electoral systems, and as such might account for the common observation that the Australian Senate is somewhat less partisan than the House of Representatives. The Australian House is elected on the basis of the alternative vote, a nonproportional system that is designed to ensure that the winning candidate in each constituency gets a majority of its votes. Under it, the voter ranks the candidates in order of preference, and if no candidate receives a majority on the first count, then the second choices of the candidate with the fewest votes are distributed among the others. The redistribution continues until a candidate has a majority. Theoretically the winner might be the second or third choice of most voters, although in fact the winner is usually the first choice. The Australian House of Representatives is as partisan as the Canadian House of Commons.

The purpose of this brief analysis is to show that the enhancement of democratic inclusiveness in the federal system through the establishment of an elected Senate is by no means a simple matter. Enthusiasts of Senate reform need to consider very carefully what kind of representation they hope election will produce, and craft their proposal accordingly. In the meantime, neither the federal government nor the provincial governments (except Alberta) have shown much enthusiasm for the idea of an elected Senate. The federal governing party is no more eager to establish an elected competitor to itself than are the provinces. Since Confederation, only the Reform Party (and its successor, the Alliance) has undertaken a sustained campaign for change in the form of an elected, equal, and effective body – the so-called Triple-E Senate. In fact, this campaign bore some fruit during the negotiations on the failed Charlottetown Accord, when the idea of an elected Senate came to life in a version that featured six senators per province and one per territory, plus an unspecified number of Aboriginal senators.

Long-time observers of Canadian politics were startled to see that the Quebec government evidently was prepared to buy into a proposal that would have had the effect of reducing its representation in the Senate. Startled, that is, until the rest of the deal was revealed. In exchange for going along with the proposed Senate, Quebec demanded and got agreement that the province's share of seats in the House of Commons would not fall to less than 25 percent of the total number of seats, irrespective of the province's population. Thus the very legislature traditionally designed to reflect the principle of representation by population would do so no longer (J. Smith 1995, 77-85). Further, it was agreed that the provinces could decide on their own how to elect their senators: directly by the provincial voters or indirectly by the provincial legislatures. The betting was that Quebec would take the indirect route and require the National Assembly to elect the province's senators. Finally, the new Senate would possess a thirty-day suspensive veto over taxing and spending measures rather than the full veto that it has now. Although an elected body, it would be less powerful legally than the Commons, being unable to thwart a government's budgetary plans.

Despite the failure of the accord, its proposal on the Senate is highly instructive even now in delineating what is possible in terms of reforming that venerable body. Election is possible, although it might require the inclusion of a wrinkle or two on different kinds of election from province to province. Even equal representation of the provinces is a possibility, although by no means a necessity. However, the trade-off is the power of the body. In the Charlottetown exercise, the federal and provincial governments were prepared to concede an equal and elected Senate but not one as powerful as the existing body, which possesses, after all, a veto on measures sent to it from the House of Commons. (The fact that the proposed Senate featured only two Es, equal and elected, but not the third E, effective, was a major reason why the Reform Party campaigned against the Charlottetown Accord in the referendum that was held on it.) Had it been armed with the veto, the Charlottetown Senate would have looked like the American Senate, and that prospect simply is not in the cards. To reiterate, the federal government, sustained by a majority in the House of Commons, and the provincial governments are unlikely to cooperate in establishing a powerful competitor to themselves.

The issue of Aboriginal representation in a reformed Senate was left unresolved in the Charlottetown proposal but the possibility was kept open. The benefits of such inclusion would consist not only in enabling Aboriginal representatives to speak to the full range of issues that face the country, and not just issues that are relevant to their communities, but in enabling non-Aboriginals to hear them. The ordinary Canadian who is not an Aboriginal has virtually no opportunity to hear voices that are restricted to the confines of internal governmental meetings. Moreover, since many Aboriginal communities are territorially based, representing them in the Senate is consistent with the principle of territorial representation that is used there. Should such representation prove unwieldy because of the number of these communities, then ways could be found to group them together for the purpose of selecting senators. However, the prospect of double representation arises. Members of these communities might find themselves being represented by the senators of the provinces in which the community is located as well as by Aboriginal senators. Conversely, Aboriginals who live in urban areas and are not members of land-based Aboriginal communities are unlikely to benefit from the additional representation of such communities. In short, Aboriginal representation on the basis of territory in a reformed Senate raises some thorny complications for Aboriginal individuals, and for the representation of the provinces and the territories.

Alternatively, Aboriginal representation can be conceptualized in terms of identity as opposed to territoriality. From time to time mention is made of the possibility of representing nonterritorial identities in elected assemblies. Nonterritorial identities might include Aboriginal as well as the indicators of gender, ethnicity, or sexual preference. Undoubtedly ways could be found to approach such a task. In fact, in the provision in the Charlottetown Accord on Senate representation, some of the provinces stated that they would require that half of their seats be guaranteed to women although they offered no indication of how they would execute such a guarantee. A similar type of offer could be made to Aboriginal communities. Another possibility is to adopt an electoral system more hospitable to the prospects of minority candidates than the single-member plurality system in use in the House, most probably a proportional system – and then leave it at that. In other words, decline to specify representative categories and instead let the electoral system in conjunction with the political parties do the work.

It is worth emphasizing that a Senate that represents nonterritorial identities is *not* the norm in federal systems. In the final analysis, federalism is largely a territorial thing. The second houses – the senates – of the central governments of federal systems everywhere except Canada are regarded as houses in which the members of the federation are directly represented. (Let us recall that the appointed Canadian Senate was intended to represent the interests of the wealthy, although it is organized on the basis of provincial/regional representation.) The representation of the members is a crucial condition of the territorial integrity of the system as a whole, which is incidentally why land-based Aboriginal communities need to be attached to the federal system – fast. The role of the provinces in the Canadian system is already so pronounced, however, that it hardly seems urgent to construct a Senate to give them more representation, despite the solid arguments made by people like Gibbins.

If the objective is inclusiveness, that is, to get more elected representatives from a broader swath of society in the Senate, then the best strategy is a body, the members of which are elected on the basis of a different electoral system from the House and on a province- and territory-wide basis. Such a body would almost certainly function as a much needed counterweight to the government-dominated House of Commons, an additional bonus. The Senate should be treated as the upper house in a parliamentary system of government – which is how it was conceived at Confederation – as well as an upper house in a federal system of government.

To summarize thus far, the factors to be juggled in the reform of the Senate are election, the number of senators elected from each province and territory, or each "region," and the powers of the body. They can be stitched together in a dizzying number of ways, each fraught with controversial consequences for the key players. Nevertheless, the main political consideration is that the power of the Senate is bound to be measured in relation to the power of the governing party in the House of Commons and of the provincial and territorial governments. Obviously then the task of reform is complicated and sensitive. It suffices to make the point that an elected Senate – surely a federal institution par excellence – is a more inclusive Senate. It would involve Canadian voters in its establishment, and add more elected representatives to the institutions of the federal government. But that still leaves Aboriginal representation nowhere.

A different idea for Aboriginal representation in the central government flows from the concept of a third order of government, which appeared in the Charlottetown Accord and then was dealt with at length in the 1996 report of the Royal Commission on Aboriginal Peoples (RCAP). The accord contained a proposal to entrench in the Constitution the Aboriginal peoples' "inherent right of self-government within Canada." Although subject to the Canadian Charter of Rights and Freedoms, this inherent right would have been tantamount to the recognition of a constitutionally secured order of government that could be developed but never erased. In the RCAP report, this idea was pursued mostly in connection with Aboriginal self-government. There was little discussion of it in the context of the institutions of the federal government, although a third chamber of Parliament was mentioned. RCAP held that such a chamber could address matters that are relevant to Aboriginal peoples by offering advice on bills sent to it from the House of Commons and the Senate, by initiating legislation, and by exercising an oversight function in relation to the administration of existing laws. RCAP's third chamber was conceived as being restricted to Aboriginal business. But Aboriginal business is not necessarily a narrow concept or even an easily defined one. Thus the establishment of a third chamber might well have the effect of injecting a fresh level of discourse into the country's political debates in general, and not simply on Aboriginal issues.

The third chamber is also a workable institution for the representation of urban Aboriginals and Métis who are not necessarily attached to a land-based Aboriginal community. As mentioned already, such individuals are not likely to benefit directly from the incorporation of land-based Aboriginal communities into the world of the federal, provincial, and territorial governments. Now they do not get representation as "aboriginal peoples of Canada" (to use the language of the Constitution Act, 1982) in the House of Commons, but instead simply as Canadian voters. The election of representatives to the third chamber would fulfill this purpose for them. The drawback of the idea is the likelihood that it would be wildly unpopular with any federal government, and even with non-Aboriginals, because of the perceived unwieldiness of a third chamber.

The decision-making processes at the national level probably seem cumbersome enough to the governing party and to many Canadians without adding another chamber. That and the unorthodoxy of a three-level legislature are enough to put paid to the idea. Anyway, a better way to deal with Aboriginal representation is through executive federalism.

INCLUSIVENESS AND EXECUTIVE FEDERALISM

Since executive federalism is the modus operandi of intergovernmental relations, it is worth asking whether it can be made more inclusive. Is it possible to expand the charmed circle of governments? As discussed earlier, the key actors are the federal government and the provincial governments, or the two levels of government empowered independently of one another under the Constitution. The territorial governments are often included in meetings of officials of these governments, although they do not have the same status as the provincial governments, being still highly dependent on Ottawa. Then there are the Aboriginal governments and the municipal governments.

At issue is whether and how to attach the Aboriginal governments to executive federalism. Under the logic of federalism, the conclusion is hard to avoid that territorially based communities with their own self-governing powers should join the club of governments. The fact that the self-governing powers might vary from those of, say, the provinces, does not negate the principle – the conjunction of territory and legal powers – on which membership in the federal system is based. In addition to principle, the practical reason for inclusion is the need for some element of coordination in what goes on across the country. There is a large number of Aboriginal nations, many of which are tiny, and there is variation in the type of governance in which these nations are engaged. The challenge is how to handle the variety in terms of making connections with the existing system of executive federalism. But this is a matter of institutional mechanics and therefore not at all insoluble. One possibility is the establishment of an Aboriginal federation of governments, which in turn sends delegates to the meetings of the other governments. And not just the meetings that include the federal, provincial, and territorial government but also the regional meetings, like those of the Western provinces or the

Atlantic provinces. This is a practical option that would require more organizational effort on the part of Aboriginal leaders than the government leaders.

Another, more ambitious option is to accomplish the same thing – the inclusion of Aboriginal leaders in the processes of executive federalism – by institutionalizing executive federalism. The institutionalization of executive federalism is exactly what the federal government itself proposed in 1991 in *Shaping Canada's Future Together,* one in a long line of documents leading to the proposed Charlottetown Accord. In *Shaping Canada's Future Together,* the federal government proposed an elected Senate and the establishment of a Council of the Federation. The elected Senate was to include Aboriginal representation. The proposal on the Council, on the other hand, said nothing about Aboriginal representation. Instead, the Council was to be composed of ministerial representatives of the federal, provincial, and territorial (Nunavut was not in existence) governments. The purpose of the Council was to deal with issues that involve intergovernmental coordination and collaboration, specifically economic issues.

The Council was conceived in conjunction with the objective of enhancing the country's economic union. Under the Constitution, a clause enjoins the free flow of goods between the provinces. In *Shaping Canada's Future Together,* the federal government proposed to strengthen and modernize the clause on the economic union by expanding it to include labour, capital, and services as well as goods; and by assigning Parliament a new power to legislate on the efficient functioning of the economic union. However, any such legislation was to be contingent on provincial approval as defined by the general amending formula, that is, at least seven of the provinces representing 50 percent of the population. The provinces were to vote in the Council of the Federation. In addition, the Council was empowered to vote on guidelines for fiscal harmonization and coordination, and to make decisions on the use of Parliament's power to spend money on new Canada-wide shared-cost programs and conditional transfers in areas of exclusive provincial jurisdiction (Canada 1991, 42).

Clearly the general idea behind the Council was to improve inter-governmental relations by taking the existing processes of executive federalism and institutionalizing them in a formal body, the existence of which, incidentally, the federal government was prepared to entrench in the Constitution. Specific kinds of federal legislative proposals would need the support of the Council before they could be placed before Parliament. There are echoes of the German Bundesrat in the Council to the extent that the German body is composed of ministerial delegates of the land governments. There are also echoes of the proposal of a provincially appointed Senate contained in a discussion paper published in 1982 by the Alberta government. But the key is that neither Canada's nor Alberta's proposal envisaged such a body to include Aboriginal representatives. And yet the Council of the Federation is certainly a perfect body for such representation, because it is meant to represent governments for specific economic purposes.

One of the critical claims made by Aboriginal leaders is their need to deal with non-Aboriginals on a government-to-government basis. Given the complexity of government operations in a federal-provincial-territorial-Aboriginal federation, what could be more desirable and useful than an institution that houses their governmental representatives together to consider federal economic policies that directly affect their administrations? It would work for urban Aboriginals attached in some fashion to a land-based Aboriginal government and for Métis with their governmental organizations. There are problems, to be sure, not the least of which is the number of self-governing, land-based Aboriginal communities; this particular problem would need to be resolved by some sort of streamlined system of representation. Nevertheless, the Council, or something like it, could play a much-needed role in the coordination of intergovernmental relations as well as being an equally needed forum in which Aboriginal leaders contribute directly to the political life of the federation.

The municipalities present a more difficult case for inclusion in federal political institutions precisely because they are the creatures of the provinces, lacking independent standing under the Constitution.

The provinces would seem unlikely to welcome their presence, especially were it to lead to conflict between them and the municipalities or to complicate their relationship with the federal government. Further, there are too many municipal-level governments to make inclusion an option. Finally, the provincial governments would undoubtedly argue that they represent the concerns of the cities wherever those concerns bear upon the issues at hand. Certainly they do under the terms of the Constitution. Nevertheless the size of the populations of cities like Toronto, Vancouver, and Montreal presents an issue of scale that will not go away, but in fact only deepen. These cities are metropoli, or city states, that dwarf the size of the populations of some of the provinces.

It is tempting to conceive of the entry of the cities into a body like the Council of the Federation. However, even the great cities lack the very thing needed for admission into the circle of executive federalism, which is a set of independent powers vouchsafed them under the Constitution. That being so, change will probably need to take place within the provinces themselves. If there is a growing impression that the cities and their concerns are not represented adequately in the system, then that is because the cities and their concerns are not represented adequately in the provincial legislatures. It is often argued that rural areas are overrepresented in many provincial legislatures. Such overrepresentation can be corrected by amendments to the electoral system. Any more radical changes, such as the reconfiguration of provincial boundaries or the establishment of new provinces to take account of the "city states," must await agitation from within the provinces.

The Case for Change: Participation

In terms of participation, one political process that bears heavily on the federal system is thus far closed to almost all of the participants. That is the selection of the federally appointed judiciary: the judges of the supreme courts and appellate courts of the provinces and the judges of the federally established courts, including the Supreme Court.

As with the Senate, so with the federal judiciary, the members of which are appointed by the governor general on the recommendation of the prime minister and hold office until the age of seventy-five. The merits of this system are said to be keeping the court out of an unseemly public political battle each time an appointment is made; keeping the court out of partisan politics, period; permitting the prime minister to achieve a balance among types of individuals on the court; and keeping the court connected to public opinion in a broad sense by virtue of the fact that an elected representative, the prime minister, has the power of appointment. These merits are worthy of consideration, although possibly overstated. For example, although the battle over appointments is not public, it still takes place behind the scenes and is probably as unseemly there as it might be in public. The issue here, however, is whether the federal principle suggests that others be included officially in the selection process.

There is a longstanding argument to the effect that the provinces ought to be involved in the selection of judges, who serve as the "umpire" of the constitutional battles between the federal government and the provincial governments. The same logic applies to the territorial governments and to the Aboriginal peoples. It has been supplemented more recently by the argument that diverse voices ought to be heard in the matter, an argument given added impetus by the arrival of the Canadian Charter of Rights and Freedoms. Should the logic of these arguments be accepted then the issue is how to amend the current selection process. Behind this question looms the example of the United States.

There the president nominates individuals to serve on the federal courts, including the Supreme Court. The Judiciary Committee of the United States Senate holds public hearings in which it not only queries the nominees of the president but also votes on them, thereby determining their fate. In Canada the suggestion has been made that candidates nominated by the prime minister ought to be similarly interviewed in public hearings held by a parliamentary committee. But which committee? No one suggests that the Senate as it stands now ought to be involved, although some have argued that an elected Senate might very well serve such a purpose. This argument is compelling because it is both a democratizing step and a way of including the provincial and territorial representatives in the process. Other possibilities include a committee of the House of Commons or a joint Senate-Commons committee.

Then there is the issue of whether to empower the committee to vote the nominees up or down, as the Americans do. Elected representatives who get to pose questions to prospective Supreme Court judges are not likely to want to stop there but instead to agitate to vote on them. Since the governing party (or parties in the event of a coalition government) is normally assigned a majority of the members of parliamentary committees, the government's nominee is safe. There might, however, be a minority government or a coalition government. Should the government's nominee run into trouble in the committee hearings, the nomination would have to be withdrawn. The government would not want to risk a negative vote. Incidentally, there is nothing wrong with such a scenario. It simply signals that a controversial nominee lacks widespread support among committee members, in which case the government needs to produce a new candidate who has good support. In the system of responsible government, the fate of a prime minister's judicial nominee is bound to be regarded as a matter of confidence on which the prime minister expects the full support of his caucus.

As this exercise makes clear, something seemingly as simple as enabling the included to participate more meaningfully in important decisions is not simple at all. The combination of the parliamentary system and federalism ensures complications. Nevertheless, it is time to reconsider the process of the selection of the judges of the Supreme Court, and possibly the other federal courts. Participation means just that – participating in important decision-making processes. The appointment of judges is an important decision-making process that

is now monopolized by the prime minister. There is no real accountability, unless the accountability mechanism of the general election is
held to suffice. However, heretofore no election has been fought on
the selection of judges. By enabling others to participate in the
process, the accountability of the government for its judicial nominees would be strengthened immediately, and the judiciary itself
would be subjected to some much-needed public scrutiny. Indeed, a
brisk brush with public scrutiny would be a salutary exercise for
eager candidates for the bench. Besides, Canadians, who pay the bills,
are entitled to see what they get in return. It is elitist beyond belief to
suggest that prospective judges be insulated from public inspection.
Most important of all is the prospect of elected representatives participating in something that matters.

The Case for Change: Responsiveness

In the federal system, the responsiveness of the governments to the
citizens is affected directly by governmental capacity to discharge the
responsibilities assigned to them under the Constitution. The capacity at issue is financial. A government might choose not to respond to
citizens who lobby for some policy or service for political, administrative, or technical reasons. However, without the financial where-
withal there is no choice to make.

It has long been observed that under the Canadian Constitution,
the responsibilities and the financial powers of the federal government and the provincial governments are not well matched.
Parliament is assigned an impressive array of legislative responsibilities and full powers of taxation. The provincial legislatures are
assigned costly legislative responsibilities, among them education,
health, and welfare, and limited powers of taxation. They are restricted to direct taxation. The reasons for the situation are rooted in the
circumstances of the mid-nineteenth century, when governments

relied largely upon excise taxes imposed on goods imported into the country, and licensing fees. At Confederation, the legislative responsibilities thought to require the most money, like defence or transportation systems such as railroads that cross provincial boundaries, were assigned to Parliament, as was the full power of taxation. By contrast, the responsibilities thought to require the least money, like municipal infrastructure or welfare (then a private matter), were assigned to the provinces, along with the one power of taxation – direct taxation – then hardly ever used. The income tax was a twentieth-century tax.

One of the great changes in the twentieth century was the growth in public spending on health, welfare, and education, which are provincial matters. The need for the provinces to rely on direct taxes like the corporate and personal income tax appears to have worked well in this respect, since these came to be the taxes most relied upon as the century wore on. The federal government could also levy these taxes, however, and in any event there was an urgent argument for it to play the principal role, namely, the national economy and the need for a consistent tax infrastructure in which the economy could grow. Further, the federal government was largely responsible for the growth in social spending following the Second World War, when liberal-democratic governments everywhere established the foundations of welfare states in which the citizens could rely on the government to provide for their basic needs from cradle to grave.

Since the federal government lacks the jurisdiction under the Constitution to administer social programs on its own, it needed to collaborate with the provincial governments that do have the jurisdiction. There were exceptions. For example, the Constitution was amended in 1940 to enable the federal government to establish a program of insurance for the unemployed. For the rest it was a matter of working with the provinces to establish new programs, like health care, for which the provinces were expected to share some of the costs. But the capacity of the provinces to share the costs was and remains uneven. The resulting problem is how to maintain comparable levels of social programs from province to province in the light of the economic inequality among them.

The economic inequality of the provinces is profound, spanning the distance between the economies of Ontario and PEI, and everything in between. Yet under the Constitution, PEI has the same legislative responsibilities as Ontario. As a response to this problem, the federal and provincial governments developed the concept of equalization based on the revenue streams available to the provinces. Under the complex equalization formula, dollars are recycled from "have" provinces to "have-not" provinces. Nevertheless, the problem of uneven financial capacity persists. A poorer province like Newfoundland and Labrador is simply unable to contribute as much on a per capita basis to any program as a wealthier province like Alberta. As a result, the quality of social programs varies from province to province. This is especially so in health care. The Romanow Commission on health care that reported in November 2002 highlighted the widening gap in the type and quality of medical services available from province to province.

In Atlantic Canada, Nova Scotia and Newfoundland and Labrador are frustrated particularly by their inability to use offshore oil and gas resources to move from the have-not to the have category. Both provinces signed offshore agreements, known as the Atlantic Accord, in 1985, designed to define the federal-provincial management of the sector, including the distribution of revenues between the governments (Royal Commission 2003, 17). Now they find that the equalization formula claws back revenues that the provinces would otherwise receive under the accord. In other words, they are unable to take advantage of the windfall of the oil and gas offshore – they are trapped.

According to some analysts, the solution to the problem is to "rebalance" the federation, and to bring the taxing and spending powers of both levels of government into line. What they mean is that the provinces should have access to more taxes in order to fund their constitutional responsibilities. Common sense suggests that such a solution would have a decentralizing effect in the federation, since it would strengthen the role of the provinces while diminishing the role of the federal government. The desirability of further decentralization is much debated. The vast technical and economic literature on the issue is far beyond the scope of this study to review. However, greater access to taxation is clearly more beneficial for governments that preside over large economies than tiny ones.

Rebalancing is a way of clarifying and thereby enhancing the responsiveness of governments to citizens. When combined with the economic inequality of the provinces, however, the result would surely be to worsen the inequality, which is hardly the desired outcome. The inequality is the crucial sticking point, and a major reason for the federal government's role in maintaining some semblance of comparability in social programs across the country. In recognition of this point, some analysts have suggested that there ought to be fewer provinces, particularly in Atlantic Canada.

The provinces in Atlantic Canada are among the economically weakest in the country. The three Maritime provinces are also the smallest geographically. Occasionally the idea has been trotted out of Maritime union, under which the three would be merged into one larger province (Smith 1996). The arguments are that one government is cheaper than three, that efficiencies of scale would be realized in the administration of programs, and that costly competition for the same business dollars would be eliminated. Predictably the union proposal collapses as soon as it is made, since no political constituency in the Maritime region has the remotest interest in it. That leaves the current constitutional framework, which specifies ten provinces that are unevenly equipped to deal with the legislative responsibilities that are assigned to them. Under this framework it is hard to see how to strengthen the responsiveness of the governments to the citizens while at the same time maintaining the minimum in terms of national standards of social services.

In terms of the Atlantic provinces, however, there is the idea of a virtual region, in which they act as if they are a region by integrating many of their regulatory regimes, especially regulations that affect businesses, transportation systems, licensing practices, and even the provision of some government services. This slow process of unification from the bottom, or the ground up, as it were, is already under way. It was given an impetus in the wake of the Free Trade Agreement signed with the United States in 1988, which spurred a dramatic increase in trade between that country and the Maritime provinces, and by the more recent efforts of the Canadian governments to remove internal barriers to trade. While the political systems of the four provinces are as isolated from one another as ever, their economies are stronger and more integrated than before. Should this trend continue, the region could become less dependent on the rest of Canada and at the same time more responsive to its citizens.

The Atlantic Institute for Market Studies (AIMS) is pursuing the idea of a virtual economic region that includes not just the Maritime provinces, southern Quebec, Newfoundland and Labrador, but as well the northeastern United States, in particular, northern New England and northern New York State. AIMS calls this putative region Atlantica. AIMS conceives of Atlantica as a natural economic region in terms of market-based economics, liberated since 1988 by the federal government's adoption of free trade with the United States, and later the United States and Mexico (AIMS 2002). While the think tank has kept its focus on the economy, developing proposals designed to strengthen the region as an economic unit, it also seeks to educate the general public to think in regional rather than provincial terms.

Conclusion

As outlined here, only a few changes can be made to the federal structure as such to enhance the democratic features of inclusiveness, participation, and responsiveness. On inclusiveness, the primary requirement is to democratize the Senate. As it stands now, the Senate is a lost democratic opportunity. It is also a confused body: some perceive the Senate to be a federal institution while others perceive it to be a parliamentary institution. If the Senate is to be a federal institution, then it has to represent the provinces, the territories, and the Aboriginal communities that are land-based. If it is to be a parliamentary institution, then it can be used to represent nonterritorial identities. The addition to the system of a body like the Council of the Federation would permit the Senate to be reconceived as a parliamentary rather than a federal institution.

For Aboriginal peoples as well as the provinces and the territories, the most interesting idea to date for representation in the central government lies in the establishment of something like the Council of the Federation as proposed in *Shaping Canada's Future Together* (Canada 1991). As conceived in that document, the Council is an entrenched body that stands at the apex of the system of intergovernmental relations. It crystallizes executive federalism in an institutional format. As adapted here, the suggestion is that it include delegations from Aboriginal governments. Their inclusion would strengthen its capacity to assist in the coordination and harmonization of public policies that require the collaboration of all of the governments. The economic, social, and political activities of Aboriginal governments cannot be expected to proceed in a fashion that is somehow isolated from those of the rest of the governments, particularly the provincial governments. Some ways need to be found to enable the delegates of the various governments of the Aboriginal communities to join the meetings of the other governments and to interact consistently with them on an ongoing basis. An institution like the Council might perform this function.

Instead, a somewhat different body has materialized. At the Annual Premiers' Conference (APC) in Charlottetown in July 2003, it was agreed to establish a permanent Council of the Federation composed of provincial and territorial leaders that would pursue the development of common positions on matters of national importance, like health care and federal-provincial financial relations. The idea was fleshed out at the meeting of the premiers in October in

Quebec City, and in December 2003 the provincial and territorial premiers signed the Founding Agreement of the Council of the Federation. The objectives of the council are to strengthen interprovincial-territorial cooperation; to exercise leadership on national issues of importance to the provinces and territories; to promote relations between governments based on respect for the Constitution and the diversity of the federation; and to promote transparency in government operations (Quebec 2004, 28).

The realization of the idea of the Council is a significant event, not least because it is championed by the premier of Quebec, Liberal Jean Charest, whose government was elected in April 2003. Jean Charest is the first committed federalist to lead the province since 1994. In the provincial election, he urged the need for greater cooperation in the conduct of Canadian federalism and to that end proposed the establishment of a permanent executive committee of the federal and provincial governments. The mandate of the committee would include matters related to the economic and social union in Canada, and international agreements that bear on provincial jurisdiction (Quebec Liberal Party 2001). Aficionados of these matters would have seen in the proposal some echoes of the Council in *Shaping Canada's Future Together,* which is not terribly surprising given that Charest was at the time a member of the federal government that issued that document.

At the July 2003 meeting of the APC, Premier Charest was prepared to go along with the other provincial and territorial leaders and settle for a council that leaves the federal government out, at least for now. Moreover, it must be stressed that the Council does not include the leaders of the Aboriginal governments. Nevertheless, should the Council prove to be a useful and workable body from the standpoint of its members, then it might grow to include both federal and Aboriginal leaders. Only time will tell. In the meantime, it is striking to see the Quebec government, for so long fixed on the sovereignty option, changing course and instead pursuing a leading role in the creation of a new institution of federalism that might well become more inclusive than is now anticipated.

Once the institutional structure of the government is made more inclusive, then participation is enhanced for the obvious reason that the included can get to participate. Participation itself, however, is about the things the included do. One thing that is federally related is the selection of the federally appointed judges, including the judges of the Supreme Court of Canada, the umpire of the federal system. Now the process essentially is in the hands of the government, in particular the prime minister, who gets to make the final decision about appointments. The process might well be opened up to include members of Parliament who scrutinize the government's nominees. They can do this in a committee of the House of Commons, or a joint (reformed) Senate-House committee. The point is simply that the selection of the judges of the country's high court bears directly on the federal system in light of the Court's role in determining disputes between the governments, and for that reason participation in the selection process needs to be broadened, but in a democratic way with the inclusion of elected representatives.

Finally there is the issue of responsiveness in the federal system. The chief mechanism for enhancing the responsiveness of the system is doubtless to balance spending capabilities with legislative responsibilities such that the citizens know easily which level of government to hold accountable for what. The trouble with the rebalancing idea, however, is that it runs smack into the economic inequality of the provinces, which was the main reason for the drift toward imbalance in the first place. The poorer provinces cannot afford the social programs that they and the other governments deem appropriate in this day and age. They need to rely on dollars from Ottawa, dollars that Ottawa in turn raises from the economies of the prosperous provinces.

Any notion of tackling the economic inequality of the provinces by diminishing their number so that there are fewer, larger provinces seems a complete political impossibility at this time. An alternative idea exists of a virtual region, at least in the Maritime provinces and Newfoundland and Labrador. One benefit of this idea is to finesse the formidable political obstacles that block any proposal that involves the union of the provinces in the region. At the very least, a virtual union might enhance the prosperity of the region. Over time, it might lead to a change in thinking about the desirability of different political arrangements.

CHAPTER 7

✦ Federalism privileges the territorial organization of political and governmental life.

✦ The great cities lack the very thing needed for admission into the circle of executive federalism, which is a set of independent powers vouchsafed them under the Constitution.

✦ It is time to include parliamentary committees in the process of selecting the judges of the Supreme Court of Canada.

✦ The Atlantic provinces should act as a "virtual region," with integrated regulatory systems and the coordinated delivery of social services.

THE NEED FOR CHANGE

In the previous chapter it was pointed out that whenever the idea of uniting the three small Maritime provinces into one large province has been advanced, there has proven to be no political support for it in the region. This simply illustrates the point that any proposed changes to the federal system in the name of democratization need to be considered within the horizon of what is realistic in political terms. Related to this is what is realistic in constitutional terms, which raises the issue of the amending formula. It is necessary to determine which of the democratizing changes under consideration here would trigger the use of the formula. To summarize, these changes are: an elected Senate; the establishment of a Council of the Federation that includes the Aboriginal governments; a legislative role in the selection of federally appointed judges, including the judges of the Supreme Court of Canada; and virtual regionalism in the Atlantic provinces.

The Amending Formula: An Obstacle to Senate Reform

Changing from an appointed to an elected Senate appears to require the formal amendment of the Constitution. But which amending formula would apply? As outlined in Chapter 3, on Canadian federal-ism, the amending formula is actually a cluster of formulas, each made applicable to specified parts of the Constitution. For our pur-poses, the key formulas are the unanimity rule and the general for-mula. To recall, the unanimity rule requires the agreement of Parliament and the provincial legislatures to changes affecting the Crown; the senatorial floor rule, under which the provinces are enti-tled to no fewer MPs than senators; the official-language provisions of national application, such as the requirement that French and English be used in proceedings in Parliament and the National Assembly of Quebec; the composition of the Supreme Court of Canada; and the amending formula itself. Obviously these matters are held to be so important that only the highest degree of consensus – unanimity – is sufficient to trigger formal change in the constitu-tional provisions governing them.

On the face of things, the change to an elected Senate would not necessarily invoke the unanimity rule. It depends on the numbers. If there were no accompanying change in the number of senators assigned to each of the provinces and the territories, then election would require agreement under the less onerous general formula, which requires the agreement of Parliament and two-thirds of the provincial legislatures that together include at least 50 percent of the population of the provinces. Or, if the number of elected senators assigned to each of the provinces were raised, then the general for-mula would also apply. If the number assigned were lowered, then the matter changes. This can be illustrated by reference to one of the smaller provinces. Nova Scotia, for example, is assigned ten senators under the Constitution. The province is also assigned eleven districts for purposes of representation in the House of Commons – so, eleven MPs. As matters stand, Nova Scotia's representation in the House is protected under the Constitution by the number of senators assigned to it. The floor is ten, below which its representation in the House can-not fall, even if that were recommended by the size of its population. Any change in numbers that affects the senatorial floor rule invokes the requirement of the unanimity rule.

It might be responded that since election to the Senate is the democratizing idea under consideration here, the actual numbers of senators assigned to each province and territory need not be changed. That is so, in theory. Once senators are elected, however, the profile of the body as a whole is bound to be enhanced, along with its legitimacy. Once senators are elected, the number of senators per province becomes more important than ever. Currently each of the Western provinces is assigned six senators. British Columbia has fewer senators than Nova Scotia, as does Alberta. In an elected Senate, these provinces are bound to demand at least the same number of seats as Nova Scotia. Certainly the Triple-E Senate (elected, equal, and effective) remains a popular option in Western Canada, and therefore the region's political leaders are likely to back it, or at least some version of it (Laycock 2002, 27).

However, why would Nova Scotia agree to reduce its representation in the Senate to six senators? Any reduction in the number of senators is unappealing on its own terms, and would also lower the floor that protects its representation in the House. That would also fall to six. Nova Scotia might consider a reduction to six – and did in the Charlottetown Accord – if each province were assigned six under the principle of equal provincial representation. In effect it would be trading its protected level of seats in the House for equal representation in a body that might become a more important partner in Parliament than it is now. But such a change affects the senatorial floor rule in the Constitution, which requires the unanimity formula.

Of course it is possible to think in terms of a larger Senate – perhaps in conjunction with a larger House – and thereby avoid the dreaded senatorial floor rule and the unanimity rule and instead meet the less strict test of the general formula. Not so. In order to see why, it is necessary to turn back the clock to the 1995 referendum on sovereignty held in Quebec, in which the secessionist option backed by the government of the province missed the mark by the smallest margin imaginable. The night of the count, there were times when it seemed liked the secessionists would win and presumably take the province out of the federation. For federalists the experience was unnerving, to say the least. In the weeks following the referendum, the federal government understandably sought strategies to placate the government of Quebec, and one such strategy involved the amending formula.

Under the general formula, with its two-thirds plus 50 percent rule, in principle it is possible to amend the Constitution without the consent of one of the large provinces, like Quebec or Ontario. Politically speaking it is hard to imagine that any federal government would do such a thing. Nevertheless, in the effort to reassure Quebec on the point, in early 1996 the federal government tabled an amendment bill in the House of Commons designed to assign to Quebec – the Quebec government would say restore to Quebec – a veto over constitutional amendments, period. Under the terms of the Act Respecting Constitutional Amendment, the federal government is required to gain specified regional approvals before submitting to the House a resolution to amend the Constitution. As drafted initially, the act counted four regions: Ontario and Quebec were each treated as regions in their own right, plus Western Canada and Atlantic Canada. Following the negative reaction of British Columbia and Alberta to being lumped together in the Western category, this was quickly changed to five regions, British Columbia being made a region in its own right, like Ontario and Quebec. For its part, Alberta was assuaged by being placed with Manitoba and Saskatchewan in a Prairie region in which consent is defined as the agreement of two provinces, the population of which is at least 50 percent of the population of the region as a whole. This effectively gives Alberta a regional veto. In the four-province Atlantic region, consent is also defined as the agreement of two provinces that together include at least 50 percent of the population of the region as a whole.

The upshot of the Act Respecting Constitutional Amendment is effectively to transform the general formula into a unanimity rule. Any amendment to the Constitution that requires the use of the general formula now needs to meet the test of this federal statute, which effectively assigns a veto to British Columbia, Alberta, Ontario, Quebec, and two Atlantic Canadian provinces that together include 50 percent of the population of the region as a whole. The provinces that matter politically have a statutory veto. Now it is true that a veto under this federal statute is not the same as a veto under the Constitution. Parliament can repeal any of its statutes. However, it is hard to imagine the circumstances under which a federal government would seek to disturb this particular law.

One way or another, then, the Canadian governments have managed to produce a state of sclerosis when it comes to the formal amendment of the Constitution. Amendment is so arduous that Canadians often refer to the desirability of such informal methods of constitutional change as the development of conventional ways of doing things, the use of intergovernmental agreements, or the ongoing interpretation of the Constitution by the courts in the course of the determination of legal disputes. Would informal change help when it comes to the election of senators? Possibly. In Alberta, the one province devoted to the idea of senators being elected in province-wide elections, such events have been held. For the most part, the federal government has ignored them and proceeded with its own appointments of senators. (The lone exception occurred in 1990, when Prime Minister Mulroney appointed elected senator-in-waiting Stanley Waters to the Senate.) There is nothing to prevent the federal government from adopting an elected "senator" as its own appointee. Yet once it took that step, it would be politically difficult to reverse direction. Provincial electorates would expect to choose candidates for Senate seats whenever vacancies arose. This is the kind of extra-constitutional development that can force what amounts to constitutional change.

Practical Reforms

Fortunately, the three remaining proposals to democratize the federal system do not require any formal amendment procedures, at least not if deftly handled. But it is worth reviewing them just to be sure. These proposals are the establishment of a Council of the Federation that includes representatives of Aboriginal governments; a legislative role in the selection of federally appointed judges, including judges of the Supreme Court of Canada; and virtual regionalism in the Atlantic provinces. In terms of the requirements of the Constitution, the tricky one is the Council of the Federation.

In *Shaping Canada's Future Together* (Canada 1991), the federal government proposed to entrench the Council in the Constitution. Certainly that would require the use of the general formula. On the other hand, the powers to be assigned to the Council amount ultimately to the power to vote up or down the federal government's policy proposals on the economic union as well as its proposals for new programs that fall in provincial jurisdiction. As such the Council appears to be an advisory body with teeth, in other words, a body that can turn down proposals of the federal government before they are tabled in Parliament. Arguably that is what happens now, however, in federal-provincial meetings. The federal government consults with the provinces and the territories on initiatives affecting them that it wants to pursue. The Council would be the institutional face of the process of executive federalism, which is extraconstitutional anyway. There is no need to entrench the Council in the Constitution; it could be established by federal statute.

To emphasize, executive federalism is an extraconstitutional phenomenon. Indeed, one of the fascinating paradoxes of Canadian political life is the fact that executive federalism, or the arena of intergovernmental relations, has developed outside of the Constitution. Certainly it is neither required nor even envisaged by the Constitution. If anything, the Constitution was based on the classical federal concept of "watertight compartments," meaning that the federal and provincial governments would operate in splendid isolation from one another. The Council of the Federation recently established by the provincial and territorial premiers is another extraconstitutional development and an extremely important one. But will it last? And what about Aboriginal leaders? Executive federalism is the arena in which the governments connect, and the Aboriginal governments need to be there, too. Giving this arena a permanent institutional form is not a small matter, to be sure, but neither is it a radical move. And it is compelled both by the growing complexity of intergovernmental relations and the Aboriginal governmental presence that is intertwined in those relations.

The insertion of the federal legislature into the selection of the federally appointed judges, including the judges of the Supreme Court, can be accomplished without resort to the Constitution because the Constitution requires simply that the governor general appoint the judges of the superior, district, and county courts. In practice this means that the prime minister appoints the judges. But there is nothing to prevent the prime minister from taking advice from legislative committees before presenting the nominees to the governor general. As far as the Supreme Court is concerned, one cautionary note involves its composition. Under the terms of the Supreme Court Act, 1985, three of the nine judges must come from Quebec. The reference to the composition of the Supreme Court in the list of items of which the amendment requires the use of the unanimity rule means that any change in the number of judges, including the share that hails from Quebec, would require an amendment to the Constitution. So long as the composition of the Court remains untouched in this respect, however, there is no constitutional bar to including the federal legislature in the selection of the judges.

The final proposal, of a virtual region in Atlantic Canada, is not so much a proposal as the recognition of an integrative trend that might well have an effect on the responsiveness of the governments of the region to its citizens. As the provincial economies continue to integrate with one another and the provincial governments respond to demands for streamlined regulatory systems from the business and professional sectors, the political leaders will face continual pressure to act in conformity with one another rather than competing. The Council of Atlantic Premiers that was established in May 2000 is a testament to this very point. The Council is designed to enable the premiers to develop common strategies to deal with critical issues that transcend provincial boundaries, like the economic and security issues arising out of the region's relationship with the United States, or the development of offshore oil and gas resources, or federal-provincial financial relations.

It is true that interest in regionalism has waxed and waned, and that the political circles in each of the Atlantic provinces continue to operate more or less independently of one another. Nevertheless, any regional political institution like the Council is a welcome development for the citizens of the region, and not simply because so many public policies have a regional ambit rather than a purely provincial one. It is welcome from the standpoint of the responsiveness of the provincial governments to the citizens. As a collection of competitive have-not provinces, the Maritime provinces and Newfoundland and Labrador have long been unable to respond much to the demands of their citizens. They are too busy stretching meagre tax dollars, many of which are generated in other parts of the country, to meet the minimum standards of various national programs, particularly the costliest program of all, health care.

Importantly, the federal system magnifies the problem of responsiveness rather than mitigates it. The economic weakness of the Atlantic provinces makes for a serious imbalance in the federal system that feeds back into the democratic loop in a negative way. These provinces are locked into a federal system in which, at least according to the Constitution, they are responsible for the delivery of social services at a level that they cannot afford – because the level is set by others, by the federal government and other provincial governments that are responding to the demands of their own electorates. They are responsible for meeting expectations that they cannot afford and therefore must depend on others to fulfill. But of course the expectations are only partly fulfilled, with the result that social program standards are the lowest in the country. In the eastern provinces, the responsiveness of the governments to the citizens is skewed under the federal system. And this will continue until the economy of the region strengthens sufficiently in relation to the economies of the other provinces and regions.

In the meantime, any institutional development that encourages these provinces to act politically as a region is likely at the same time to strengthen their capacity to be responsive to the citizens who live there. The reason is the old adage about strength in numbers. If the provinces are better off economically by acting together to rationalize the delivery of public services or streamline regulations applicable to the business sector, then they can do more for their citizens. If they are better off politically by acting together to develop common negotiating strategies with other governments, then they can do more for their citizens. They might be four provinces, and as provinces entitled to a variety of expensive privileges, including the maintenance of full-fledged parliamentary systems of government. But politically they could do better by counting as one province, which would require them to act as one province in the councils of executive federalism.

Conclusion

This last series of observations on the way in which the federal system can interfere with the capacity of governments to be responsive to the citizens illustrates the point that the fit between federalism and democracy is not necessarily smooth. As was noted at the very outset of this book, democrats do not establish federal systems in order to get more democracy. Democrats, and antidemocrats for that matter, wind up joining a federal system because it is the best option short of the independence that they would prefer but cannot afford. As a consequence, in many federal systems the key concern is to keep the member states or provinces in the system – to keep them from wanting to leave it.

Many in Quebec continue to express an interest in leaving the Canadian federation. To get them to think otherwise is still to be accomplished. Less extreme but equally important is the longstanding discontent with the federal system in western Canada, particularly in BC and Alberta. Unable to spearhead reform of the system, Westerners have been left to express their grievance with the system in the way that they always have: through the establishment of new political parties. The Western-based Alliance was the most recent example but it proved a dead end, and as noted previously, the party merged with the Progressive Conservatives in 2003 to form the new Conservative Party. Meanwhile, at the other end of the country, the province of Newfoundland and Labrador, still reeling from the ramifications of the débâcle in the cod fishery, gave vent to its feelings of discontent in the time-honoured Canadian fashion in April 2002 by establishing a royal commission to investigate the role of the province in the federation.

The report of the Royal Commission on Renewing and Strengthening Our Place in Canada (2003, 2) contains these startling words: "Newfoundlanders and Labradorians feel ignored, misunderstood and unappreciated by their federal government and, to a lesser extent, by other Canadians." In its recommendations, the commission avoided anything that would require the amendment of the Constitution, an exception being its support of an elected Senate with equal representation of the provinces. Instead, the commission focused on the province's need to strengthen its economy, citing an improvement in the working relationship between the federal, provincial, and territorial governments as central to that effort.

Although the demand for change in the federal system is persistent – now by one region, now by another – it has proven exceptionally difficult for the country's political leaders to generate a sufficient consensus in favour of any set of proposals. The vote against the proposed Charlottetown Accord in 1992 was a clear demonstration of the difficulty of generating the public consensus needed to implement change. As a result, the federal architecture of the country remains unchanged. The structure persists of ten provinces, plus the two territories and Nunavut; the economic inequality among the provinces and the territories continues to widen; and the dysfunctionality of the system that flows from this inequality deepens. Under the Constitution the provinces are treated as equals but in fact they are not. One cost of the dysfunctionality is the responsiveness of the governments, certainly the eastern governments, to their citizens.

Making it possible for the governments to attend to their responsibilities under the Constitution, and thereby be responsive to the citizens for those responsibilities, is a question of boundaries. As has been stressed here again and again, the federal system is territorially based. This means boundaries, which are deeply sensitive matters. Nevertheless, at some point the advisability of retaining the ten provinces needs to be raised. As far as the Atlantic provinces are concerned, consolidation is the issue. In the past the argument for consolidation has always been utilitarian, the claim being that it would permit economic efficiencies. The democratic audit undertaken here suggests that there is a democratic argument to be made as well. The federal system is structured to inhibit the realization of the third criterion of the audit, responsiveness, not to enhance it.

As matters now stand, then, Canadian federalism needs some adjustment in order to meet the democratic audit's standards of inclusiveness, participation, and responsiveness. It is inclusive, but not inclusive enough, particularly in relation to the country's Aboriginal communities. It invites participation, but is not participatory enough, particularly in relation to the role of the elected representatives in the federal Parliament. It secures responsiveness but is not responsive enough, particularly in relation to the capacity of the less prosperous provinces and territories to respond to the demands of the citizens that they discharge their responsibilities under the Constitution at the same level as the more prosperous provinces do.

As discussed above, some adjustments can be made without amending the Constitution. Others, like Senate reform, ostensibly require the formal amendment of the Constitution, although not necessarily on the issue of election. As indicated previously, the country could wind up with an elected Senate in fact although not in law. The political leaders will have to get out in front of the democratic impulse to elect senators if they want to control the process of change.

The Need for Change

This issue of the Senate is a perfect place to conclude the democratic audit of federalism. History shows that a broad consensus among Canadians is needed for any substantial changes to the federal system. It also shows how difficult it is to generate that consensus. The Senate issue, however, yields the insight that democracy can drive change in the federation. The public desire to elect senators is simply the wish for more democratic government.

Chapter 8

- Canadian governments have managed to produce a state of sclerosis when it comes to the formal amendment of the Constitution.

- The economic weakness of the Atlantic provinces makes for a serious imbalance in the federal system that feeds back into the democratic loop in a negative way.

- In many federal systems, the key concern is to keep the member states or provinces from leaving the federation.

Discussion Questions

Chapter 2: Federalism and Democracy

1 What are the key defining features of the federal system of government?
2 In what ways are the member states of the federal system equal?
3 How is it that federalism can be considered an alternative to empire?
4 In what ways is federalism thought to impede democracy?
5 What does the federal system offer to diverse democratic communities that need to coexist within the confines of one state?
6 In what ways does the rule of law serve to support democracy?
7 How does political autonomy at the local level of government encourage democratic self-rule?
8 Explain how federalism establishes a system of competitive elites. Does this help to promote democracy?
9 What is the distinction drawn by Will Kymlicka (1998) between multination federalism and territorial federalism? Is either one applicable to Canada?
10 Explain the ways in which the federal system structures the relationship between minorities and majorities.

Chapter 3: Canadian Federalism

1 How democratic is the assignment of seats to the provinces in the House of Commons?
2 At Confederation, critics of the Senate argued that it was not a federal body. Is their argument still relevant today?
3 Does the Canadian cabinet operate as a federal institution?
4 What are the "antifederal" features of the Canadian Constitution? Do they matter?
5 How can the development of such extraconstitutional institutions as first ministers' conferences or the Annual Premiers' Conference be explained?

Chapter 4: Democratic Audit of Inclusiveness in the Federal System

1 Why are territorially based communities the only ones that are represented politically in federal systems?
2 How are the cities represented in Canada's federal system?
3 What are the constitutional particulars that undergird Quebec's position in the federation?

4   Does the combination of land claim agreements and self-government agreements require that Aboriginal communities gain formal representation in the institutions of federalism?

5   Why do boundaries remain such an important condition of inclusion in the democratic process in an age of technology that ostensibly knows no boundaries?

Chapter 5: Democratic Audit of Participation in the Federal System

1   From the standpoint of citizens, is democracy more than a matter of voting in elections?

2   What obstacles does the federal system place in the way of citizens' participation in politics?

3   What are the reasons for the development of executive federalism in Canada?

4   Why does executive federalism have the effect of producing "done deals" between the federal government and the provincial governments that the public has no capacity to affect?

Chapter 6: Democratic Audit of Responsiveness in the Federal System

1   Why are institutionalized centres of opposition to the government so important in exacting the responsiveness of governments to the citizens?

2   Why are Canadian elections not as competitive as some might like?

3   What is the role of the federal system in impeding the development of competitive, national political parties?

4   Does competition between the federal government and the provincial government(s) work in favour of the citizens? Does it serve the formulation of good public policy?

Chapter 7: The Democratic Audit and Change in the Federal System

1   How compelling is the argument against change in the federal system?

2   What arguments might be made to convince the provinces of the need for reform of the Senate?

3   Is it possible to respond intelligently to urban issues without assigning the cities a guaranteed revenue stream in addition to the revenues now raised from the property tax?

4   Would a more public, inclusive process than is used now to select members of the federal judiciary jeopardize the independence of the judiciary?

5   Is further decentralization of the federal system bound to be a consequence of any attempt to bring the spending responsibilities and tax revenues of each level of government into alignment?

Chapter 8: The Need for Change

1 Why does the senatorial floor rule hamper Senate reform?

2 How and why did Parliament stiffen further the requirements of the amending formula in the wake of the Quebec government's failed referendum on independence?

3 Which would attach Aboriginal communities more closely and constructively to the federal system, an institution to house executive federalism that includes Aboriginal leaders, or a third parliamentary chamber?

4 Is it realistic to suppose that over time a "virtual region" of small provinces could transform itself into one large province?

Additional Reading

Those looking for theoretical literature on federalism should begin by consulting *The Federalist* (Madison, Hamilton, and Jay [1791] 1977), the compendium of short essays authored by James Madison, Alexander Hamilton, and John Jay in 1791 in support of the constitution drafted at the Philadelphia convention. Lord Acton's analysis of the federal system can be found in "The influence of America" (1985), while A.V. Dicey's is available in his *Introduction to the study of the law of the constitution*, 4th ed. (1893).

In the twentieth century, the leading student of the theory and practice of federalism was K.C. Wheare, who wrote the widely read text entitled *Federal government*, 4th ed. (1963). In it he maintains a technical focus on the institutions of federalism and never really discusses democracy at all. William Riker disputed the democratic origins of federal systems in his *Federalism: Origin, operation, significance* (1964). In *Federalism and constitutional change* (1956), W.S. Livingston argued that federalism is a function of societies composed of territorially based communities and a mechanism to enable them to live together peacefully. Reginald Whitaker analyzed the important relationship between federalism and democracy in *Federalism and democratic theory* (1983). Albert Breton argued the case for the democratic effect of competitive federalism in his "Supplementary statement" (1985) to the Royal Commission on the Economic Union and Development Prospects for Canada. Michael Burgess has demonstrated the democratic appeal of federalism even in allegedly unitary countries in *The British tradition of federalism* (1995). Recently T.O. Hueglin has explored the concept of treaty federalism in relation to the European Union in "From constitutional to treaty federalism" (2000). In *Multinational democracies* (2001), edited by A.-G. Gagnon and J. Tully, the relationship between federalism and issues of recognition and justice is explored.

One of the leading students of comparative federalism in the world is the Canadian political scientist Ronald Watts. His works include *Comparing federal systems*, 2d ed. (1999a), and *The spending power in federal systems: A comparative study* (1999b). Daniel J. Elazar has edited the useful *Federal systems of the world: A handbook of federal, confederal, and autonomy arrangements* (1994). Another useful work is the *Handbook of federal countries* (2002), edited by Ann Griffith. Each chapter is focused on a different country and includes a list of references for those seeking further material on the federal system there. As far as Canadian federalism is concerned, Richard Simeon has written a splendid bibliographic guide entitled *Political science and federalism: Seven decades of scholarly engagement* (2002).

For those who wish to pursue the origins of the idea of federalism in the pre-Confederation period, there is William Ormsby's *The emergence of the federal concept in Canada, 1839-1845* (1969). On the Aboriginal concept of treaty federalism, there is James (sákéj) Youngblood Henderson's "Empowering treaty federalism" (1994). For the Confederation period, a new resource on the debates in the colonial legislatures is Janet Ajzenstat, Paul Romney, Ian Gentles, and William D. Gairdner, eds., *Canada's founding debates* (1999). Regrettably there is no collection based on the debate conducted outside the legislatures in the press and in pamphlets. Those who are interested in it need to visit the national and provincial archives, where these documents are housed. Other guides to these debates include Peter Waite's *The life and times of Confederation: 1864-1867* (1962), and J. Murray Beck's *Joseph Howe*, vol. 2: *The Briton becomes Canadian, 1848-1873* (1983). Jennifer Smith's "Canadian Confederation and the influence of American federalism" (1988) compares the democratic and federal features of the Canadian Constitution in 1867 with its American counterpart. Robert Vipond's *Liberty and community: Canadian federalism and the failure of the constitution* (1991) contains an original analysis of the federal concept adopted at Confederation.

There is a rich tradition of writing on constitutional issues in Canadian federalism, and some of it bears upon democratic issues. Norman M. Rogers was an early critic of the judiciary's interpretation of the federal Constitution, as indicated by essays entitled "Government by the dead" (1931) and "The dead hand" (1934). Another was F.R. Scott, whose trenchant critiques penned before and during the Second World War are available in his *Essays on the Constitution* (1977). Both Rogers and Scott argued that the federal system had the effect of thwarting the will of the Canadian people and their elected governments. The tradition continues in the works of D.V. Smiley, *Canada in question*, 3d ed. (1980); W.R. Lederman, *Continuing Canadian constitutional dilemmas* (1981); Peter Hogg, *Constitutional law of Canada*, 4th ed. (1996); G.-A. Beaudoin, *Constitution du Canada: Institutions, partage des pouvoirs, droits et libertés* (1990); and Patrick Monahan, *Constitutional law*, 2d ed. (2002).

Governments have weighed in, striking royal commissions to study various problems of Canadian federalism. The reports of the commissions are essential reading, since they contain analyses of these problems that bear on the democratic prospects of federalism. Troubled by its inability to cope with economic and social demands during the Great Depression, the Nova Scotia government established a Royal Commission, Provincial Economic Enquiry to consider what might be done. In its report (Nova Scotia 1934), the commission recommended that Ottawa take over some social-policy fields like unemployment insurance. The federally appointed Royal Commission on Dominion-Provincial Relations issued its report in 1940. The commission held that all Canadians ought to receive similar levels of government services at roughly similar levels of taxation, and to that end recommended some adjustments to the division of powers between the two levels of government that would enhance Ottawa's position. By contrast, Quebec's Royal Commission of Inquiry on Constitutional Problems issued an elegant defence of provincial autonomy in its report in 1956.

Decades later the country was contemplating a different economic relationship with the United States. In its report in 1985 the federally appointed Royal Commission on the Economic Union and Development Prospects for Canada urged the country to consider a free-trade agreement with the United States as well as some democratic reforms to the federal system, including an elected Senate. The most recent in the line is *Our Place in Canada, the report of the Royal Commission on Renewing and Strengthening Our Place in Canada* (2003) established by Newfoundland and Labrador. The commission recommends a more collaborative approach between Ottawa and the province in such areas as the management of the fisheries.

Scholars have also produced fascinating and instructive studies of federal-provincial relations that illuminate the Canadian brand of executive federalism. There is Garth Stevenson's *Unfulfilled union*, 3d ed. (1989), and his *Ex uno plures: Federal-provincial relations in Canada, 1867-1896* (1993). In *Federal-provincial diplomacy: The making of recent policy in Canada* (1973), Richard Simeon used the framework of international diplomacy to shed light on the interaction between the federal and provincial governments. Simeon also edited *Confrontation and collaboration: Intergovernmental relations in Canada today* (1979), which contains the important and provocatively entitled essay by D.V. Smiley, "An outsider's observations of federal-provincial relations among consenting adults." J.S. Dupré's "Reflections on the workability of executive federalism" (1985) is essential reading on the dynamics of the system. In his *Regional ministers: Power and influence in the Canadian cabinet* (1991), Herman Bakvis used the role of the political minister for a given province or region to illuminate yet another aspect of executive federalism.

Alan Cairns probed the relationship between executive federalism and democracy in the case of Meech Lake in "Citizens (outsiders) and governments (insiders) in Canadian Constitution-making: The case of Meech Lake" (1988). Simeon and D.M. Cameron directly target executive federalism and democracy in "Intergovernmental relations and democracy: An oxymoron if ever there was one?" (2002).

Finally, there are many interesting interpretive treatments of Canadian federalism that bear on democratic issues, like Pierre Elliott Trudeau's *Federalism and the French Canadians* (1968), in which he discussed the concept of self-government. A.I. Silver raised issues associated with federalism and democracy in *The French-Canadian idea of Confederation, 1864-1900* (1982). Roger Gibbins analyzed the ramifications of federal institutions like the elected US Senate in *Regionalism: Territorial politics in Canada and the United States* (1982). P.H. Russell looked at the relationship between democracy and legitimate constitutional foundations in *Constitutional odyssey: Can Canadians become a sovereign people?* (1992). Samuel V. LaSelva explored democratic inclusiveness in *The moral foundations of Canadian federalism: Paradoxes, achievements, and tragedies of nationhood* (1996). David Thomas's *Whistling past the graveyard: Constitutional abeyances, Quebec, and the future of Canada* (1997) demonstrates the significant role of implicit as opposed to explicit political understandings in the conduct of Canadian federalism. Recently in *Straight talk: Speeches and writings on Canadian unity* (1999), Stéphane Dion has made the argument that federalism promotes a public philosophy of tolerance, which in turn enhances the quality of democratic politics.

Works Cited

Statutes

An Act Respecting the Constitution Act, 1982, R.S.Q. L412.

An Act Respecting the Exercise of the Fundamental Rights and Prerogatives of the Quebec People and the Quebec States, 2003, R.S.Q. E-20.2.

Canada Health Act, R.S. 1985, c. C-6, s. 23.

Canada-Newfoundland and Labrador Atlantic Accord Implementation Act, RSNL 1990, c. 2.

Clarity Act, 2000, c. 26.

Constitution Act, 1867 (U.K.), 30 & 31 Vict., c. 3.

Constitution Act, 1982, being Schedule B to the Canada Act 1982 (U.K.), 1982, c. 11.

Nunavut Act, 1993, c. 28.

Supreme Court Act, 1985, c. S-26.

Cases

Delgamuukw v. *British Columbia*, [1997] 3 S.C.R. 1010.

R. v. *Powley*, [2003] 2 S.C.R. 207.

Reference re Objection by Quebec to Resolution to Amend the Constitution, [1982] 2 S.C.R. 793.

Reference re Resolution to Amend the Constitution, [1981] 1 S.C.R. 753.

Reference re Secession of Quebec, [1998] 2 S.C.R. 217.

Severn v. *The Queen* (1878), 2 S.C.R. 70.

Other Sources

Acton, John Emerich Edward Dalberg. 1985. The influence of America. In *Essays in the history of liberty: Selected writings of Lord Acton*, ed. J. Rufus Fears, vol. 1, 198-212. Indianapolis: Liberty Classics.

AIMS (Atlantic Institute for Market Studies). 2002. Putting Atlantica back together again: The international northeast economic region in the context of North American integration. 26 February. <www.aims.ca/commentary/atlantica. html>. (2 May 2003).

Ajzenstat, Janet, Paul Romney, Ian Gentles, and William D. Gairdner, eds. 1999. *Canada's founding debates*. Toronto: Stoddart.

Alberta. 1982. *A provincially appointed Senate: A new federalism for Canada*. Alberta government discussion paper on strengthening Western representation in national institutions. Edmonton.

Baier, G. 2002. Judicial review and Canadian federalism. In *Canadian federalism: Performance, effectiveness, and legitimacy,* ed. Herman Bakvis and Grace Skogstad, 24-39. Don Mills, ON: Oxford University Press.

Bakvis, Herman. 1991. *Regional ministers: Power and influence in the Canadian cabinet.* Toronto: University of Toronto Press.

Bakvis, Herman, and Laura G. MacPherson. 1995. Quebec block voting and the Canadian electoral system. *Canadian Journal of Political Science* 28(4): 659-92.

Beaudoin, G.-A. 1990. *Constitution du Canada: Institutions, partage des pouvoirs, droits et libertés.* Montreal: Wilson et Lafleur.

Beck, J. Murray. 1983. *Joseph Howe.* Vol. 2, *The Briton becomes Canadian, 1848-1873.* Montreal: McGill-Queen's University Press.

Breton, A. 1985. Supplementary statement. In *Report,* Royal Commission on the Economic Union and Development Prospects for Canada, vol. 3, 486-526. Ottawa: Supply and Services Canada.

Browne, G.P., ed. 1969. *Documents on the Confederation of British North America.* Toronto: McClelland and Stewart.

Bueckert, Dennis. 2004. Martin promises billions for cities. 2 February. <http://cnews.canoe.ca/CNEWS/Canada/2004/02/02/333>. (19 March 2004).

Burgess, Michael. 1995. *The British tradition of federalism.* London: Leicester University Press.

Cairns, Alan. 1968. The electoral system and the party system in Canada, 1921-1965. *Canadian Journal of Political Science* 1(1): 55-80.

—. 1988. Citizens (outsiders) and governments (insiders) in Canadian Constitution-making: The case of Meech Lake. *Canadian Public Policy* 14: 121-45.

—. 2000. *Citizens plus: Aboriginal peoples and the Canadian state.* Vancouver: UBC Press.

Canada. 1991. *Shaping Canada's Future Together.* Ottawa: Minister of Supply and Services Canada.

—. 2003. Backgrounder: Industry and business: Working with industry and business to address climate change. 12 August. <www.climatechange.gc.ca>. (26 November 2003).

Canada.comNews. 2002. Anderson defends climate pact. *Times Colonist* (Victoria), 16 May, 1.

Canadian Press. 2002. Activists blast new panel on medicare disputes. *Globe and Mail,* 26 April, A7.

Chase, Steven. 2002. Cut energy use, Ottawa says. *Globe and Mail,* 24 October, A1.

Chase, Steven, Richard Mackie, and Patrick Brethour. 2002. Divulge plan on Kyoto, angry Eves tells Ottawa. *Globe and Mail,* 2 October, A5.

Chase, Steven, and Dawn Walton. 2002. Goals too vague and uneven, critics say. *Globe and Mail,* 25 October, A8.

Commission on the Future of Health Care in Canada. 2002. *Building on values: The future of health care in Canada.* Saskatoon: Commission on the Future of Health Care in Canada.

Courtney, John C. 2001. *Commissioned ridings: Designing Canada's electoral districts.* Montreal: McGill-Queen's University Press.

—. 2004. *Elections.* Vancouver: UBC Press.

Cross, William. 2004. *Political parties.* Vancouver: UBC Press.

Desnomie, Stuart. 2003. City proposes Aboriginal strategy. *The Manitoban.* 10 September. <www.umanitoba.ca/Manitoban/20030910/ne_01.html>. (24 March 2004).

Dicey, A.V. 1893. *Introduction to the study of the law of the constitution.* 4th ed. London: Macmillan.

Dion, Stéphane. 1999. *Straight talk: Speeches and writings on Canadian unity.* Montreal: McGill-Queen's University Press.

Docherty, David. 2004. *Legislatures.* Vancouver: UBC Press.

Dunfield, Alison. 2002. PM signs Kyoto treaty. <www.globeandmail.ca>. 16 December.

Dupré, J.S. 1985. Reflections on the workability of executive federalism. In *Intergovernmental relations,* ed. R. Simeon, 1-32. Toronto: University of Toronto Press.

Elazar, Daniel. 1985. Federalism and consociational regimes. *Publius: The Journal of Federalism* 15(2): 17-48.

—, ed. 1994. *Federal systems of the world: A handbook of federal, confederal, and autonomy arrangements.* 2d ed. Essex, UK: Longman.

Elections Canada. 2002. *Representation in the House of Commons of Canada.* Pamphlet. Ottawa: Elections Canada.

Federal Interlocutor for Métis and Non-Status Indians. 2003. Urban Aboriginal Strategy. <www.pco-bcp.gc.ca/interlock>. (24 March 2004).

Finer, Herman. 1932. *The theory and practice of modern government,* vol. 1. London: Methuen and Co. Ltd.

Gagnon, A.-G, and J. Tully, eds. 2001. *Multinational democracies.* Cambridge: Cambridge University Press.

Gibbins, Roger. 1982. *Regionalism: Territorial politics in Canada and the United States.* Toronto: Butterworths.

Greater Vancouver Regional District. 2003. Aboriginal population growth far outpaces the non-Aboriginal population. Planning Department. <www.gvrd.bc.ca/publications/file.asp?ID=505>. January. (24 March 2004).

Greene, Ian. 2005. *The courts.* Vancouver: UBC Press.

Griffith, Ann, ed. 2002. *Handbook of federal countries.* Montreal: McGill-Queen's University Press.

Henderson, James (sákéj) Youngblood. 1994. Empowering treaty federalism. *Saskatchewan Law Review* 58(2): 241-329.

Hogg, P. 1996. *Constitutional law of Canada.* 4th ed. Toronto: Carswell.

Howe, Joseph. 1865. The botheration scheme – No. 1. Halifax *Morning Chronicle,* 11 January, 1-2.

—. 1909. Mr. Howe on Confederation. In *The Speeches and Public Letters of Joseph Howe,* ed. Joseph Andrew Chisholm, vol. 2, 468-92. Halifax: Chronicle Publishing Company Limited.

Hueglin, T.O. 2000. From constitutional to treaty federalism. *Publius: The Journal of Federalism* 30: 137-53.

Hurley, James Ross. 1996. *Amending Canada's Constitution: History, processes, problems and prospects.* Ottawa: Minister of Supply and Services Canada.

King, Preston. 1982. *Federalism and federation.* Baltimore: Johns Hopkins University Press.

Kymlicka, W. 1998. *Finding our way: Rethinking ethnocultural relations in Canada.* Don Mills, ON: Oxford University Press.

LaSelva, Samuel V. 1996. *The moral foundations of Canadian federalism: Paradoxes, achievements, and tragedies of nationhood.* Montreal: McGill-Queen's University Press.

Laskin, Bora. 1964. "Peace, order and good government" re-examined. In *The courts and the Canadian Constitution,* ed. W.R. Lederman, 66-104. Toronto: McClelland and Stewart.

Laycock, David. 2002. *The new right and democracy in Canada: Understanding Reform and the Canadian Alliance.* Don Mills, ON: Oxford University Press.

Lederman, W.R. 1981. *Continuing Canadian constitutional dilemmas.* Toronto: Butterworths.

Livingston, W.S. 1956. *Federalism and constitutional change.* Oxford: Clarendon Press.

McGee, Thomas D'Arcy. 1865. Speech at Cookshire, County of Compton, December 22, 1864. In *Speeches and addresses chiefly on the subject of British-American Union,* 122-40. London: Chapman and Hall.

Madison, James. [1791] 1977. No. 39. In *The federalist,* ed. Jacob E. Cooke, 269-77. Franklin Center, PA: Franklin Library.

Madison, James, Alexander Hamilton, and John Jay. [1791] 1977. *The federalist,* ed. Jacob E. Cooke. Franklin Center, PA: Franklin Library.

Manfredi, Christopher P. 2001. *Judicial power and the Charter: Canada and the paradox of liberal constitutionalism.* 2d ed. Don Mills, ON: Oxford University Press.

Manning, Preston. 1992. *The new Canada.* Toronto: Macmillan.

Mendelsohn, Matthew. 2002. Four dimensions of political culture in Canada outside Quebec: The changing definition of brokerage and the definition of the Canadian nation. In *Canada: Canadian political culture(s) in transition,* ed. Hamish Telford and Harvey Lazar, 51-82. Montreal: McGill-Queen's University Press.

Milne, D. 1991. Equality or asymmetry: Why choose? In *Options for a new Canada,* ed. R.L. Watts and D.M. Brown, 285-308. Toronto: University of Toronto Press.

Monahan, Patrick. 2002. *Constitutional law.* 2d ed. Toronto: Irwin Law.

Morton, F.L., and Rainer Knopff. 2000. *The Charter revolution and the court party.* Peterborough, ON: Broadview Press.

Nevitte, Neil. 1996. *The decline of deference.* Peterborough, ON: Broadview Press.

Nova Scotia, Royal Commission, Provincial Economic Enquiry. 1934. *Report.* Halifax: King's Printer.

Ormsby, William. 1969. *The emergence of the federal concept in Canada, 1839-1845.* Toronto: University of Toronto Press.

Pedersen, Rick. 2002. Councillors tout virtues of Kyoto pact. Canada.comNews. *Times Colonist* (Victoria), 2 June.

Province of Canada. 1865. *Parliamentary debates on the subject of the Confederation of the British North American provinces.* Quebec: Parliamentary Printers.

Quebec. 2004. *The Council of the Federation: A first step towards a new era in intergovernmental relations in Canada.* Government of Quebec, Secrétariat aux affaires intergouvernementales canadiennes, Ministère du conseil executive.

Quebec Liberal Party. 2001. *A project for Quebec: Affirmation, autonomy and leadership: Final report.* Montreal: Special Committee of the Quebec Liberal Party on the Political and Constitutional Future of Quebec Society.

Reguly, Eric. 2002. Polluters win on Kyoto Canada-style. *Globe and Mail,* 28 November, B2.

Riker, W.H. 1964. *Federalism: Origin, operation, significance.* Boston: Little, Brown.

Rogers, Norman M. 1931. Government by the dead. *Canadian Forum* 12: 47.

—. 1934. The dead hand. *Canadian Forum* 14: 421.

Royal Commission of Inquiry on Constitutional Problems. 1956. *Report.* Quebec City.

Royal Commission on Aboriginal Peoples. 1996. *Report of the Royal Commission on Aboriginal Peoples.* 5 vols. Ottawa: Ministry of Supply and Services.

Royal Commission on Dominion-Provincial Relations. 1940. *Report.* 3 vols. Ottawa: King's Printer.

Royal Commission on Electoral Reform and Party Financing. 1991. *Reforming Electoral Democracy,* vol. 1. Ottawa: Minister of Supply and Services Canada.

Royal Commission on Renewing and Strengthening Our Place in Canada. 2003. *Our Place in Canada.* St. John's: Office of the Queen's Printer.

Royal Commission on the Economic Union and Development Prospects for Canada. 1985. *Report.* 3 vols. Ottawa: Minister of Supply and Services Canada.

Russell, Peter H. 1992. *Constitutional odyssey: Can Canadians become a sovereign people?* Toronto: University of Toronto Press.

Savoie, Donald J. 1999. *Governing from the Centre: The concentration of power in Canadian politics.* Toronto: University of Toronto Press.

Scott, F.R. 1977. *Essays on the Constitution.* Toronto: University of Toronto Press.

Senate. 1961. *Report.* Ottawa: Queen's Printer.

Silver, A.I. 1982. *The French-Canadian idea of Confederation.* Toronto: University of Toronto Press.

Simeon, Richard. 1973. *Federal-provincial diplomacy: The making of recent policy in Canada.* Toronto: University of Toronto Press.

—. 2002. *Political science and federalism: Seven decades of scholarly engagement.* Kingston, ON: Institute of Intergovernmental Relations, School of Policy Studies, Queen's University.

—, ed. 1979. *Confrontation and collaboration: Intergovernmental relations in Canada today.* Toronto: Institute of Public Administration of Canada.

Simeon, Richard, and D.M. Cameron. 2002. Intergovernmental relations and democracy: An oxymoron if ever there was one? In *Canadian federalism: Performance, effectiveness, and legitimacy,* ed. Herman Bakvis and Grace Skogstad, 278-95. Don Mills, ON: Oxford University Press.

Simeon, Richard, and Ian Robinson. 1990. *State, society and the development of Canadian federalism.* Studies commissioned by the Royal Commission on the Economic Union and Development Prospects for Canada, vol. 71. Toronto: University of Toronto Press.

Smiley, D.V. 1979. An outsider's observations of federal-provincial relations among consenting adults. In *Confrontation and collaboration: Intergovernmental relations in Canada today,* ed. R. Simeon, 105-13. Toronto: Institute of Public Administration of Canada.

—. 1980. *Canada in question.* 3d ed. Toronto: McGraw-Hill.

Smith, A.J. 1866. Untitled article. Saint John *Morning Freeman,* 30 June, 1.

Smith, D.E. 1995. *The invisible crown: The first principle of Canadian government.* Toronto: University of Toronto Press.

—. 2003. *The Canadian Senate in bicameral perspective.* Toronto: University of Toronto Press.

Smith, Jennifer. 1983. The origins of judicial review in Canada. *Canadian Journal of Political Science* 16(1): 115-34.

—. 1988. Canadian Confederation and the influence of American federalism. *Canadian Journal of Political Science* 21(3): 443-63.

—. 1995. The unsolvable constitutional crisis. In *New trends in Canadian federalism,* ed. Francois Rocher and Miriam Smith, 67-90. Peterborough, ON: Broadview Press.

—. 1996. The economic case for political union in Atlantic Canada. In *Has the time come? Perspectives on cooperation,* ed. Maurice Mandale and William Milne, 9-19. Fredericton, NB: APEC and University of New Brunswick.

—. 2002. Informal constitutional development: Change by other means. In *Canadian federalism: Performance, effectiveness, and legitimacy,* ed. Herman Bakvis and Grace Skogstad, 40-58. Don Mills, ON: Oxford University Press.

Smith, Jennifer, and Herman Bakvis. 2002. Canadian general elections and the money question. In *Political parties, representation, and electoral democracy in Canada,* ed. William Cross, 132-44. Don Mills, ON: Oxford University Press.

Stevenson, Garth. 1989. *Unfulfilled union.* 3d ed. Toronto: Gage.

—. 1993. *Ex uno plures: Federal-provincial relations in Canada, 1867-1896.* Montreal: McGill-Queen's University Press.

Tanguay, A. Brian. 2002. Political parties and Canadian democracy: Making federalism do the heavy lifting. In *Canadian federalism: Performance, effectiveness, and legitimacy,* ed. Herman Bakvis and Grace Skogstad, 296-316. Don Mills, ON: Oxford University Press.

Thomas, David M. 1997. *Whistling past the graveyard: Constitutional abeyances, Quebec, and the future of Canada.* Don Mills, ON: Oxford University Press.

Trudeau, Pierre Elliott. 1968. *Federalism and the French Canadians.* Toronto: Macmillan.

Vipond, Robert. 1991. *Liberty and community: Canadian federalism and the failure of the Constitution.* Albany: State University of New York Press.

Waite, Peter. 1963. *The life and times of Confederation: 1864-1867.* Toronto: University of Toronto Press.

Watts, Ronald L. 1999a. *Comparing federal systems.* 2d ed. Montreal: McGill-Queen's University Press.

—. 1999b. *The spending power in federal systems: A comparative study.* Montreal: McGill-Queen's University Press.

Wheare, K.C. 1963. *Federal government.* 4th ed. London: Oxford University Press.

Whitaker, R. 1983. *Federalism and democratic theory.* Kingston, ON: Institute of Intergovernmental Relations, Queen's University.

White, Graham. 2005. *Cabinets and first ministers.* Vancouver: UBC Press.

Wilkins, Martin. 1867. *Confederation examined in the light of reason and common sense and the B.N. Act shown to be unconstitutional.* Halifax: N.p.

Young, Lisa, and Joanna Everitt. 2004. *Advocacy groups.* Vancouver: UBC Press.

Index

Printed and bound in Canada by Friesens

Copy editor: Sarah Wight

Text design: Peter Ross, Counterpunch

Typesetter: Artegraphica Design Co. Ltd.

Proofreader: Gail Copeland

Indexer: Christine Jacobs